STATE BOARD FOR
TECHNICAL AND
COMPREHENSIVE EDUCATION

BEAUFORT TEC

LRC

LEARNING RESOURCE CENTER
BEAUFORT TECHNICAL COLLEGE
BEAUFORT, SOUTH CAROLINA 29902

BEHIND THE SCENES
OF
INTERNATIONAL FINANCE

PAUL EINZIG

ARNO PRESS
A New York Times Company
New York • 1978

Editorial Supervision: MARIE STARECK

Reprint Edition 1979 by Arno Press Inc.

Reprinted by permission of The Macmillan Press.
This book is copyright in all countries which are
signatories to the Berne Convention.

Reprinted from a copy in The Newark Public Library

INTERNATIONAL FINANCE
ISBN for complete set: 0-405-11200-9
See last pages of this volume for titles.

Manufactured in the United States of America

Library of Congress Cataloging in Publication Data

Einzig, Paul, 1897-1973.
   Behind the scenes of international finance.

   (International finance)
   Reprint of the 1931 ed. published by Macmillan,
London.
   1. Finance, Public--History. 2. Economic history--
1918-1945. 3. Finance, Public--France--History.
I. Title. II. Series: International finance
(New York, 1979-   )
HJ236.E5 1979   332.4'5   78-3912
ISBN 0-405-11216-5

BEHIND THE SCENES OF
INTERNATIONAL FINANCE

MACMILLAN AND CO., Limited
LONDON · BOMBAY · CALCUTTA · MADRAS
MELBOURNE

THE MACMILLAN COMPANY
NEW YORK · BOSTON · CHICAGO
DALLAS · ATLANTA · SAN FRANCISCO

THE MACMILLAN COMPANY
OF CANADA, LIMITED
TORONTO

BEHIND THE SCENES
OF
INTERNATIONAL FINANCE

BY

PAUL EINZIG

AUTHOR OF "THE FIGHT FOR FINANCIAL SUPREMACY,"
"INTERNATIONAL GOLD MOVEMENTS,"
"THE BANK FOR INTERNATIONAL SETTLEMENTS," ETC.

MACMILLAN AND CO., LIMITED
ST. MARTIN'S STREET, LONDON
1931

COPYRIGHT

PRINTED IN GREAT BRITAIN
BY R. & R. CLARK, LIMITED, EDINBURGH

PREFACE

THE object of this book is to show that the economic calamity from which the world is suffering has been mainly the result of the fight that has been carried on since the war behind the scenes of International Finance. Its main contention is that the financial warfare conducted by France in order to acquire political power over Europe has largely contributed to the development of the economic depression since 1929, and has been the direct cause of its accentuation during the second half of 1931 into a crisis without precedent.

Until recently, it was widely assumed that the economic troubles which had been increasing almost without interruption since the Wall Street crash, were merely a recurrence of the "cyclic" crisis familiar to pre-war generations. Its exceptional violence and its rapid extension since May 1931 have, however, made everybody realise that we are confronted with an entirely abnormal situation. The present crisis seems to be fundamentally different from those which occurred periodically every eight or nine years throughout the nineteenth century. On every previous occasion the crisis brought into motion corrective tendencies which resulted in a readjustment within a comparatively short time. The reason why these forces have not become operative on this occasion is that the political factor has been interfering with the normal tendencies which would have otherwise brought about a recovery.

The man in the street is vaguely aware that "something must be fundamentally wrong somewhere"; but in his eagerness to trace the root of the evil he is inclined to follow false trails, and becomes the easy victim of doctrinairism and propaganda. Hence the number of those, who regard the present world calamity as a proof of the inefficiency of the capitalist economic system and as an indication of its impending doom, is increasing steadily as the crisis grows worse. Others regard the gold standard as the main source of all our troubles, while many people are inclined to fix the responsibility upon the banking system, and especially upon those eternal scapegoats, the international financiers. In reality, the imperfections of capitalism, the gold standard, and the international financial system would not, in themselves, have aggravated the present crisis beyond the dimensions experienced in the crises of pre-war days. The machinery of the economic system, which worked, on the whole, satisfactorily before the war, is still virtually the same. Though the work it has to do has, since the war, become more difficult, it could none the less have satisfied the greater demand upon it, but for the interference of the politicians with its work. If an engine, designed for peaceful and productive work, is used for destructive and bellicose purposes, it can hardly be blamed for being unable to fulfil its normal task.

It is the ambitious and destructive policy pursued by France in the sphere of International Finance that has paralysed the machinery of our economic system. The author's contention is that it is the French reparations policy which has prevented the financial consolidation of Europe since the war; that it was the French gold-hoarding policy which brought about the slump in commodity prices, which in turn was the main cause of the economic depression; that it is the unwillingness of France to co-operate with other nations which has aggravated the depression into a violent crisis; and that her unwillingness to co-operate is still the principal obstacle to an economic recovery.

On the ruins of the wealth, prosperity, and stability of other nations France has succeeded in establishing her much desired politico-financial hegemony over Europe. She has attained this end by means of a carefully devised and skilfully executed scheme of financial warfare which has inflicted suffering and misery upon five continents. Part of the facts relating to this warfare is a matter of general knowledge, but a considerable part of the action has evolved behind the scenes of International Finance, hidden from the eyes of the public.

It is only with extreme reluctance that the author— who has great admiration for the French nation, and realises how grave is the problem of safeguarding its security against a German aggression—has decided to place his facts before the public. The primary object of his book is not to deliver an indictment of France, but to plead for international financial disarmament, in the interests of real peace and prosperity. The only means of achieving this object is to make public opinion realise the devastating effect of her financial warfare, and, with that in view, it has unfortunately been inevitable that some hard facts should be stated and some grave accusations made against French policy. Had the financial warfare come to a conclusion, the author would share the view of those who think that the sooner this inglorious chapter of post-war History is forgotten the better for everybody concerned. Since, however, the battle behind the scenes of International Finance still continues unabated, and, at the moment of writing, the French attitude still constitutes the main obstacle to an economic recovery of the world, there is no justification for withholding the facts from public discussion. By blocking the way to a reasonable and equitable settlement of the reparations problem, and by withholding from the rest of mankind the financial resources she has hoarded, France continues to inflict sufferings upon the world. Her statesmen appear to believe that they have the right, in the name of the *sacro egoismo di patria*, to bring the world to the verge of ruin, if they imagine that in so doing they can safeguard the national soil against German aggression. Yet it would be in France's own interests for her people and her leaders to realise that, in pursuing such a destructive policy, they will not attain their end, as any safeguards provided by her financial victory must be temporary and illusory.

It is only fair to point out that the statesmen, officials, and financiers, who took part in the elaboration or execution of the French plan of financial warfare can not be blamed individually for its consequences. They were prompted by patriotic motives, and their policy was backed by the predominant majority of the French nation. In fact, any other policy would have met with insuperable opposition from both Parliament and electorate. But so long as such misguided patriotism prevails there is no hope for an international understanding. The sooner France realises that her policy must inevitably lead to complete political isolation the sooner will genuine co-operation be established for the solution of the world crisis.

To-day, it is perhaps not too late. By adopting a policy of genuine co-operation, even at this eleventh hour, France would earn the world's gratitude, and past grievances would be forgotten. To-morrow, it may perhaps be too late to prevent a complete economic collapse, from which France herself could not possibly remain immune. Or, perhaps, it may be too late for her to avoid the consequences which History shows to follow surely and inevitably upon political isolation.

P. E.

20 BISHOPSGATE, E.C.,
October 1931.

CONTENTS

	PAGE
PREFACE	v

CHAPTER I
INTRODUCTORY 1

CHAPTER II
FINANCIAL DIPLÓMACY 13

CHAPTER III
FRENCH REPARATIONS POLICY 22

CHAPTER IV
FRANCE'S FINANCIAL RECOVERY 28

CHAPTER V
ORIGIN OF FRANCE'S GOLD STOCK 37

CHAPTER VI
GOLD IN INTERNATIONAL POLITICS 45

CHAPTER VII
FIGHT FOR SUPREMACY 59

CHAPTER VIII
FRANCE AND THE WORLD CRISIS 66

CHAPTER IX
The Creditanstalt Affair 75

CHAPTER X
The German Crisis 82

CHAPTER XI
The Climax in Central Europe 91

CHAPTER XII
London's Crisis 99

CHAPTER XIII
France v. Italy 108

CHAPTER XIV
Europe's Financial Dictator 116

CHAPTER XV
Suspension of the Gold Standard . . . 122

CHAPTER XVI
France v. the United States 131

CHAPTER XVII
Balance-sheet of the Financial War . . . 141

CHAPTER XVIII
Future Prospects 150

CHAPTER I

INTRODUCTORY

THE Armistice of November 1918 put an end to military operations, and the Treaty of Versailles restored political peace. Yet the war between nations was not over—only its scene was transferred from the battlefields to the domains of International Finance. Reparations claims, war debts, loans, credits, gold movements, and foreign exchange operations have assumed the rôle hitherto played by divisions, battleships, and air squadrons. Finance Ministers, Treasury officials, Central Bank Governors, and international bankers have taken the place of Generals and Admirals. The new kind of warfare, which has been carried on since 1919 behind the scenes of International Finance, is less spectacular than was the Great War, but hardly less destructive. It does not destroy life, but inflicts misery upon mankind. Its victims are the millions of unemployed. Its devastated areas are the abandoned factories, the unsaleable stocks of produce, burnt or rotting, the closed doors of insolvent banks, and the vanished prosperity of all classes and nations. It has destroyed immense amounts of wealth and has reduced the standard of living throughout the world. It has checked the progress of mankind, and has brought about a lasting set-back which threatens to jeopardise the very roots of modern civilisation.

The general public is at last beginning to take an interest in international financial developments—the depreciation or appreciation of the currency, gold imports and exports, foreign loans and credits, or the Bank for International Settlements. It is gradually becoming aware that all these events are closely linked with international politics, and that the greatest economic crisis of modern history has been mainly the result of the transfer of hostilities to the financial sphere after the war. There is a steady increase in the number of those who realise that, although many other factors may have shared the responsibility for the depression of 1929–1931, its accentuation into a violent crisis in the summer of 1931 is to be attributed almost exclusively to the financial warfare conducted by France for political ends. But there is as yet no current in international public opinion sufficiently strong to suppress the financial warfare in the same way as postwar Pacifism has rendered virtually impossible a repetition of 1914.

For the present at least, international peace, in the political sense of the term, is safely established in Europe, not so much through the adherence of most Governments to the League Covenant, the Locarno Pact, the Kellogg Pact, and a number of other international agreements, as through the strong and increasing antipathy of international public opinion to any attempt to change the existing state of affairs by resorting to force. Unfortunately, the treaties of nonaggression and the genuine pacific sentiments of the nations—without which these treaties would be mere scraps of paper—are directed solely against war in a political and military sense. So long as armies and navies are at rest and normal diplomatic relations are maintained, the letter of these pacts is fulfilled. There is no pact, however, to prevent any country from waging war against its political opponents with the weapons of International Finance. If France were to occupy the most insignificant of German frontier villages there would be a world-wide outcry of indignation, and the aggressor would be confronted with the joint action of the signatories of the Locarno Pact. She has been at liberty, however, without running any such risk, to pursue a financial policy aiming at the destruction of the financial power of her ex-enemies and ex-allies, even though the damaging effect of such a financial aggression has been a multiple of any possible damage that could be caused by a military occupation. There are no international treaties to prevent such financial aggressions, and, until recently, international public opinion has ignored their very existence. It is easy to understand the reason for this flaw in post-war Pacifism. The effects of a military aggression are concrete and obvious, those of a financial aggression abstract and concealed. The political motives which actuate financial events are most difficult to ascertain; in the highly complicated system of International Finance, the factors at work are often intangible, and their function is often obscured by innumerable cross-currents.

French foreign policy has taken full advantage of the one-sidedness of International Pacifism, and has quickly adapted its line of action to the changed situation. In order to understand the French endeavour to achieve political ends by financial means, and its clash with British policy, it is necessary to bear in mind that the relations between Diplomacy and International Finance in the Anglo-Saxon and the continental countries are fundamentally different. As a general rule, British foreign policy serves the financial interests of the nation, while in continental countries, and particularly in France, financial interests are used as a means to further political ends. The explanation lies in part in the difference in character and mentality between the two nations, and this again is merely the consequence of fundamental circumstances. The comparative security of Great Britain from armed aggression enables her in foreign policy to concentrate upon the maintenance of conditions suitable for the improvement of her standard of living. The same may be said, even more definitely, of the United States. Thanks to their geographical position, the two Anglo-Saxon nations are not under the necessity of concentrating so much attention on self-defence as are continental nations which, ever since the collapse of the Roman Empire, have lived in terror of foreign invasion. The latter have always regarded as the principal task of their foreign policy the creation of political and economic conditions likely to assist them in the task of safeguarding themselves against military aggression. With that end in view, they have always aimed at reducing their potential adversaries to a state of military, political, economic, and financial inferiority. Being comparatively self-sufficient, their prosperity has not depended to such an extent as that of Great Britain upon the prosperity of the rest of the world. The foreign policy of Great Britain, on the other hand, has aimed at creating and maintaining political, economic, and financial stability abroad, as this is the condition of prosperity for the British Isles. Admittedly, this constructive spirit in British foreign policy has been mainly inspired by the "selfish" desire to raise and maintain the standard of living of the British nation, but at the same time it has been in accordance with the real interests of mankind as a whole.

The same constructive spirit which has inspired Great Britain's foreign policy throughout History, has characterised also the policy of the London financial market. The loans granted by London bankers to foreign countries before the war aimed at assisting the borrowers in the development of their resources, and contributed to a great extent to the increase of prosperity on the five continents. The pre-war activities of the Paris capital market, on the other hand, were inspired by, and were conducted in accordance with, the aims of the French foreign policy, the main object of which was to increase the military strength of the allies of France in case of war with Germany. The financial resources of the French investing public were placed at the disposal of Russia and the Balkan countries. Financial considerations were sacrificed to the supreme objects of French foreign policy. Nor was France by any means the only continental country to pursue this method of political finance. During the last decade or two that preceded the war, Germany was beginning to develop into a lending country of importance, and her policy in lending abroad was inspired by the same motives as that of France.

Since the war the difference between the British and French foreign policy has become even more pronounced than it was before 1914. Ever since the Armistice Great Britain has pursued a policy aiming at assisting in the economic reconstruction and financial stabilisation of the Continent. In following this goal, she has come inevitably into conflict with the French policy; which, prompted by the desire to safeguard France against a recurrence of the invasion of 1914–1918, aimed at maintaining Germany in a state of political inferiority by financial means. It has been Great Britain's aim to help all continental countries—including her ex-enemies and her rivals in the field of international trade—to become once more prosperous; for prosperity abroad has become more essential than ever to the maintenance of the standard of living in Great Britain. France, on the other hand, considered it more important than ever before to concentrate all her efforts on securing herself against a German aggression. Although defeated and disarmed, post-war Germany, with her population of over sixty millions, with her superior organising power, energy, and ambition, remained a dangerous potential enemy. France mistrusted the strength and sincerity of German Pacifism —a mistrust which, it must be admitted, was not altogether unjustified. On several occasions, concessions made by France—such as the evacuation of the Rhineland before the term of occupation actually expired— were followed by a swing towards aggressive Nationalism in Germany. This explains why a predominant section of public opinion in France has come to the conclusion that force is a better safeguard than a policy of *rapprochement*.

An explanation, however, is not necessarily an excuse. It is possible, and even probable, that the pacific tendencies that unquestionably prevailed in Germany immediately after the war would really have taken root in the minds of her population but for the aggressive policy adopted by France from the day of the Armistice. Moreover, while France may or may not have been right in distrusting her ex-enemy, she was decidedly wrong in distrusting her ex-ally. With her essentially political mentality, she was unable to understand that the British foreign policy, when aiming at the reconstruction of Germany, was not directed against her, but was merely necessitated by the peculiar economic structure of Great Britain, which rendered her prosperity largely dependent on the welfare of the rest of the world. Great Britain has, in fact, done a great deal to allay the French fears of a new German invasion. As a signatory of the Peace Treaties, Locarno Pact and Kellogg Pact, and as a member of the League of Nations, she pledged herself to support France in case of an unprovoked aggression against her. As a result of the war, moreover, British public opinion in the first few post-war years was more pro-French than at any time in History. This sentiment, while it lasted, provided in itself a most effective safeguard against German aggression. Under the guidance of shortsighted politicians, however, France has sacrificed this valuable goodwill for the illusion of security gained by the victories of her Financial Diplomacy. She showed a complete lack of understanding of the problems confronting the British nation. Her leaders may have realised that, in conducting a destructive financial warfare, they would be damaging vital British interests, and that they would alienate British sympathies, but they considered it worth their while to sacrifice Great Britain's friendship in order to attain the position of Europe's financial dictator. They imagined that this would provide better safeguards against a German aggression than would Great Britain's friendship and the moral strength of a good cause.

Neither British public opinion nor even well-informed political and financial circles were, on the other hand, able to appreciate the meaning and consequences of the nightmare of German aggression that has been weighing upon the mind of France ever since the war. They did not realise that the desperate means to which France might resort in the interests of her security, might prove of even graver danger to international economic prosperity than the maintenance of Germany in a state of economic inferiority. Had they realised it, possibly they would have proceeded more carefully with their policy of reconstruction, so as to avoid arousing the suspicions of France. Had the two nations understood each other's problems and mentality better, a formula might have been found to safeguard the interests of both. As it was, they gradually drifted apart.

French foreign policy after the war sought to obtain its political ends largely with the aid of financial weapons. The French statesmen realised that, in the changed circumstances, their aim of maintaining Germany in a state of inferiority could not be attained solely by the use of force in a political and military sense. Their last attempt to defy post-war Pacifism was the Ruhr occupation in 1923, the effects of which upon international public opinion made France realise that, in order to avoid political isolation, she would have to choose in future methods less obviously in conflict with the current pacifist attitude.

It was feared in Paris that, once the economic prosperity and financial independence of Germany was restored, she might become a dangerous opponent in spite of the restrictions imposed upon her by the Treaty of Versailles. To prevent this, the French foreign policy concentrated its efforts upon maintaining Germany in a state of economic and financial inferiority.

INTRODUCTORY

The most effective weapon in the hands of France was her reparations claims. The amount fixed by a succession of agreements was obviously in excess of Germany's capacity to pay, and all that France had to do to prevent the economic consolidation of Germany was to insist upon the execution of reparations agreements. Even though she repeatedly consented to reductions in the amounts payable, she could do so without running any risk of loosening her grip on Germany, as, notwithstanding the reductions, the burden of reparations remained still beyond Germany's capacity.

Until the end of 1926, reparations policy was practically the only weapon at France's disposal, and, formidable as it was, it appeared to be inadequate to retain Germany in a state of dependence. Thanks to the constructive Anglo-Saxon financial policy, Germany was enabled to meet her reparations liabilities with the aid of British and American loans and credits. The increasing extent to which Germany's financial stability became dependent upon the continuity of the Anglo-Saxon financial support curtailed her freedom of action, but this did not altogether satisfy Paris, for instead of becoming subject to French control, Germany was gradually coming under Anglo-Saxon influence. Thus, in order to succeed in its object, French Diplomacy had to devise further means in addition to reparations policy. Germany could not be expected to submit to French dictation so long as she could depend on financial support from Great Britain and the United States. The first task of French Financial Diplomacy was, therefore, to render impossible further assistance to Germany from Anglo-Saxon sources. This was by no means easy. Between 1919 and 1926, France had her own financial difficulties to contend with, and she was not, therefore, in a position to throw her full weight into the fight. From 1927, however, her financial recovery and the huge "fighting fund" she succeeded in accumulating enabled her to take the offensive.

The following chapters will attempt to give an account of every phase of the French struggle for financial dictatorship. It will be seen in Chapter II. that the possession of a first-rate Financial General Staff has enabled France to take advantage of the opportunities provided by the world's financial troubles. Chapter III. will explain the part played by reparations policy in the general scheme of financial warfare, and why it was in itself inadequate to bring about the desired result. In Chapter IV. is described the French financial recovery, which paved the way for her active intervention in the field of International Finance, while Chapter V. examines the origins of France's powerful gold reserves. The preliminary encounters in the fight behind the scenes of International Finance are described in the following three chapters, the last of which examines the connection between the French gold hoarding policy and the development of the international economic depression. From Chapter IX. onwards the book deals with the more dramatic phases of the financial warfare; beginning with the open clash between British and French interests over the Creditanstalt affair, it gives an account of the progress of France along the path to victory. The climax in Germany is followed by the fight for the stability of the pound, which culminated in the suspension of the gold standard in Great Britain. In Chapter XV. it is shown that this was a reverse for

French Financial Diplomacy. France's successful attempt to isolate Italy by winning over her allies is described in Chapter XIV., while Chapter XVI. explains the methods by which France sought to acquire political influence over the United States. The last two chapters give a "balance sheet" of the results obtained by France from her aggressive financial policy and their probable costs, and suggests what may be the possible course of developments in the future.

Opinion is divided as to how far the financial warfare conducted by France from 1927 to 1931 was the outcome of a premeditated Machiavellian plan, and how far it was the result of a coincidence of events favouring a French victory. Although luck may have played a certain part in the game, and France may owe her financial victory, to a certain extent, to fortuitous circumstances, nevertheless it seems highly probable that the success of her financial campaign was largely due to the supreme skill of its authors. However it may be, during the second half of 1931 France realised her ambition. Both Great Britain and the United States were eliminated as potential sources of support for Germany, and she assumed the rôle of the financial dictator of Europe.

Time alone will show whether this victory was in accordance with the real and permanent interests of France. For although, from a French point of view, it may appear justifiable to sacrifice the prosperity of the rest of the world for the security of the national soil, the question is whether in the long run French prosperity will not suffer to the same extent as that of other countries. Possibly the answer to this question is that security from aggression overshadows every other consideration. But it still remains to be seen whether a security which she hoped to obtain by sacrificing the prosperity of other nations, and jeopardising her own, will not in the long run prove to be illusory.

CHAPTER II

FINANCIAL DIPLOMACY

ALTHOUGH the association of International Politics with International Finance is not a post-war development, its significance has increased considerably since the war. Before the war there were isolated instances in which the foreign policy of certain countries made use of financial means to attain political ends. Since the war, however, the financial factor has assumed predominance in the sphere of foreign policy. This was largely due to the strong tendency towards Pacifism which followed the war. Before 1914, sabre-rattling was the principal method with which various Governments supported their diplomatic actions. Partial mobilisation, the concentration of troops near the frontiers, bellicose statements, were the weapons with which pre-war Diplomacy worked. But since the war, although they have been employed occasionally, their importance has declined. As everybody is aware that in the changed conditions none of the Governments would dare to risk another war unless it were forced into it, sabre-rattling has come to be regarded as ineffective bluff. Experience has shown that the threatening utterances of certain continental statesmen have invariably been followed by an outburst of indignation on the part of international public opinion which has eventually necessitated the withdrawal or qualification of the statements, and the offender has usually got little or no benefit from resorting to pre-war practice.

Post-war Diplomacy has adopted much more subtle means to attain its end. It works through financial channels. The complexity of International Finance provides a convenient screen for its activities. Heavy withdrawals of gold brought about by untraceable indirect methods may produce in given circumstances the same effect as did military manœuvres or threatening speeches before the war. They have the advantage of escaping the attention of pacifistic public opinion.

The trend towards Pacifism is not the only reason for the increased importance of finance in the sphere of Diplomacy. The change in the international financial situation has also been an important factor. In the comparatively normal conditions prevailing before the war, Financial Diplomacy would have had only a limited scope. Although the budgetary situation of many Governments was far from ideal, and the monetary and banking situation in some countries became rather precarious from time to time, the situation was seldom, if ever, so desperate as to induce any European Government to sacrifice its political independence for financial considerations. Doubtless, Governments were in need of loans even in pre-war days, and many countries were anxious to secure foreign capital for the development of their resources. But their requirements were not urgent. The absence of external support would have meant in most cases merely a slowing down of progress, or at worst a comparatively moderate set-back. There was keen competition between the lending centres, and although loans of a political flavour were occasionally granted both by France and Germany, these transactions did not in any way influence the external policy of the debtor Governments, which did not hesitate to accept loans from both countries and retained their political independence intact. The monetary situation was, generally speaking, stable, and most countries worked with an ample margin of gold reserves. For this reason, there was no scope for gold transactions of a political nature.

The situation has undergone a fundamental change since the war. Owing to the enormous increase of public debts and expenditure in every country, the budgetary situation has become much less stable than it was before the war. Although during the period between 1922 and 1930 most Governments claimed to have attained budgetary equilibrium, in many cases the equilibrium was more fictitious than real, and in every case its basis was rather doubtful. It was obvious that adverse circumstances could easily upset the balance. There was therefore much more likelihood of an imperative necessity for immediate financial support for a number of Governments than in pre-war days. The international monetary situation had also become much less stable. Although during the period between 1925 and 1930 a large number of countries stabilised their currencies, the situation was far from safe. Too many abnormal factors—reparations, war debts, and other international transfers of capital—were at work, and the margin of the gold reserve available for most countries to cope with emergency was highly inadequate. In such circumstances, there was every likelihood of emergencies arising from time to time in various countries which would urgently necessitate external assistance. Financial Diplomacy was thus placed in a position to save or wreck the finances of certain countries by granting or withholding support. Moreover, the currencies of most countries, debtors and creditors alike, were apt to become vulnerable, and there was ample scope for artificial interference with their stability. Before the war it was simply unthinkable that a country should have to make political concessions in order to obtain external support to balance its budget or maintain the stability of its currency. In the changed situation, however, the development came well within the bounds of practical politics.

Owing to the predominant importance of financial questions, every Government was compelled to devote much more attention to them than before the war. The international character of the problems necessitated a series of international conferences and negotiations in which financial experts played a more important part than politicians. They were, however, bound to the foreign policy of their Governments, and their expert knowledge was subordinated to diplomatic considerations.

While before the war international conferences were the business of professional diplomatists and statesmen, since the war Treasury officials and bankers have come to the fore. In every country a set of financial diplomatists has developed. Officially they do not belong to the diplomatic service, and in many cases they hold no official posts, but their services have been required regularly, and the same names have figured in the lists of participants in most of the international financial conferences. Professional Diplomacy has also been compelled to take into account the change in requirements. The days when the chief task of an Ambassador was to pay compliments to dowager Duchesses are over. Members of the diplomatic services must nowadays be as familiar with the parlours of banks as with the state rooms of palaces. They must be able to discuss questions of banking technique with the same authority as questions of international law. Diplomatic appointments are, indeed, made nowadays with special regard to the changed requirements, and those possessing a good knowledge of international financial matters stand a better chance of promotion than those who still regard diplomacy as consisting mainly of social functions. Much-coveted ambassadorial posts are usually filled with diplomatists possessing a thorough knowledge of finance. Immediately after the war there was a tendency to replace professional diplomatists in the leading posts by outsiders with financial knowledge, but subsequently members of the service in every country have acquired the knowledge necessary to enable them to hold their own.

Statesmen and politicians have also realised the necessity of interesting themselves in international financial matters. Prime Ministers can no longer afford to leave these questions to the technical expert, and to confine themselves to the management of general policy, for the simple reason that the general policy itself depends now to a very great extent upon the technical questions of International Finance.

One of the chief reasons why France has been able to rise to prominence in the sphere of International Finance and has been successful in making use of financial means to further the ends of her foreign policy is that she has possessed a first-rate personnel of financial statesmen and diplomatists. The financial warfare conducted by her was planned and executed with the utmost skill, and its results have exceeded even the most optimistic and ambitious expectations. The lion's share of the credit for the French financial victory is due to M. Poincaré. Although at the time when the decisive battles were fought he lived in complete retirement, it was his financial policy that laid the foundation of France's financial strength, and it was his spirit that inspired his successors in continuing the campaign of financial warfare. Although his successors, M. Tardieu and M. Laval, did not possess his financial genius, they were able to carry on his work, for, once the policy was inaugurated, it developed almost automatically. All that was required was an able Financial General Staff to put the policy into practice. Fortune has favoured France in this respect, as she has produced during the last few years an amazingly large number of extremely able financial experts. The names of some of them are household words in international banking circles, although they may convey nothing to the man in the street abroad or even in France. Some of them occupy a comparatively modest position, while others remain completely behind the scenes. Among those who have played an important part in putting into practice M. Poincaré's financial policy, M. Charles Farnier deserves to be mentioned first. Until October 1930 he was Director of the Movement of Funds at the French Treasury, while at present he is Deputy-Governor of the Bank of France. The present Governor, M. Moret, and his predecessor, M. Moreau, have been guided in their policy to a great extent by M. Farnier. Opinions are divided as to the part M. Quesnay, Manager of the Bank for International Settlements, has played in French Financial Diplomacy. According to some, he is an internationalist and does not satisfy the extreme wing of French Nationalists. In reality, however, he has devoted himself whole-heartedly to the French policy of expansion.

There is reason to believe that a well-known banker, the head of one of the leading Paris banks, has played a prominent part in influencing French Financial Diplomacy from behind the scenes. Although from time to time his relations with the successive Governments and with certain high Treasury officials have been rather strained, it is believed that all the time he has managed to make himself felt, directly or indirectly. While the basic idea of the French international financial expansion may have originated with M. Poincaré, its elaboration, which required a thorough knowledge of the technicalities of International Banking, is believed to have been largely inspired by this banker.

The supporters of an aggressive financial policy have succeeded in eliminating the moderate elements in the French Financial General Staff. The history of M. Caillaux's failure is a matter of general knowledge, and requires no repetition. Another prominent financial expert who was too moderate for the liking of the nationalist wing was M. Charles Rist, who believed in a policy of *rapprochement*, and, as Deputy Governor of the Bank of France, was in part responsible for the conciliatory attitude which it adopted in the summer of 1927. He was, however, eliminated from the Bank of France, and ever since he has fulfilled the functions of a financial Ambassador in Bukarest, Madrid, Angora, Vienna, etc., carrying out instructions without being able to influence the policy of his headquarters in Paris. M. Germain Martin, Finance Minister under M. Tardieu, had attempted to adopt a policy of *rapprochement* towards the end of 1930, but was also soon removed from power. Thus it came about that in the critical year of 1931 the French Financial General

Staff was entirely under the control of extreme nationalists.

One of the reasons why French Financial Diplomacy has been so exceptionally successful has been the willingness of French banks to adapt their activities to the requirements of the official policy. To some extent there is, and there should be, co-operation between banks and the authorities in every country, but in France the willingness of bankers to serve the external policy of their Government is entirely exceptional. They never hesitate to undertake a transaction if the Ministry of Foreign Affairs, or the Treasury, or the Bank of France requires them to do so, even if it appears to be against their own business interests, and they are ready to abandon any scheme, however profitable, if the authorities view it with disfavour.

Another circumstance which greatly assisted France was her influence upon the Press, not only in France, but also abroad. Although the innumerable organs of the French Press may represent as many shades of opinion in domestic politics, their attitude in matters relating to foreign politics is characterised by a remarkable degree of discipline. Even Press organs which in domestic politics are violently opposed to the Government, readily take official hints as to their attitude in matters of foreign policy. The financial warfare was actively supported by every section of the French Press, and by many foreign Press organs. The explanation of the influence of the French authorities upon foreign newspapers lies mainly in their willingness to oblige foreign Press correspondents with inside information. In this respect British authorities have only themselves to blame for being at a disadvantage through the pro-French attitude of many influential foreign Press organs, for they themselves have always adopted an attitude of extreme reserve and reticence towards publicity. Being unable to obtain information from British sources, Press correspondents were often compelled to collect from French sources such information as was obtainable. It is only natural that those Press organs which were willing to use the information received in accordance with French interests should receive favourable treatment. This explains the pro-French attitude of the Paris and Basle correspondents of many German and other foreign papers, and even of some correspondents of the English Press.

France is by no means the only country to possess able financial diplomatists. Germany, the United States, Italy, and the smaller countries, and last but by no means least Great Britain, have each had a number of extremely able financial experts at their disposal. The high officials of the British Treasury and of the Bank of England are second to none in technical knowledge, even if, generally speaking, they may not be as subtle as their French colleagues. The reason why in 1931 Britain suffered a financial defeat at the hands of France does not lie in the inferiority of the British Financial General Staff. Circumstances played into the hands of the opponent. If there is one point in which British financial diplomatists are open to criticism for their defeat, it is that they underestimated their opponents. In common with every section of British public opinion they were so utterly convinced of the unassailable strength of Britain's financial citadel that a defeat was, to them, simply unthinkable. In this respect the lesson of 1931 may prove to be useful.

CHAPTER III

FRENCH REPARATIONS POLICY

THE French financial warfare may be separated into two distinct periods, with the year 1926, when M. Poincaré succeeded in stabilising the franc, as the dividing line. Between 1919 and 1926 the unsatisfactory state of France's own finances, which brought about the depreciation of the franc, put her at a disadvantage. During that period she was unable to play an active part in International Finance, and, apart from a few isolated efforts to secure by financial means a political foothold in countries of Central and Eastern Europe, she was, on the whole, on the defensive. Her only weapon was her reparations policy—a formidable weapon indeed, and one which she did not hesitate to use extensively. While little is known about the facts relating to the activity of French Financial Diplomacy behind the scenes of International Finance, the facts of the French reparations policy are a matter of general knowledge. We do not propose, therefore, to dwell upon them at greater length than is necessary to indicate the place of reparations policy in the general strategy employed.

The main cause of the financial troubles of Europe after the war was the necessity of adjusting the terms of the Treaty of Versailles to the phraseology of President Wilson's Fourteen Points. From a financial point of view, a frankly annexationist Treaty would have done less harm than a Treaty which, while disclaiming annexationist intentions, enabled the victor to reduce and maintain the vanquished nation in a state of inferiority for an indefinite period under the pretext of collecting reparations. The result of the application of the principle laid down by President Wilson, that the Central Powers should make good the damages caused by them, was that Germany was delivered to the mercy of France for some generations to come. It was on this principle that France was able to claim and to obtain a 52 per cent participation in the proceeds of reparations. As the war was fought mainly on French soil, the material damage suffered by France was naturally far greater than that of any other nation; but her share in the total cost of the war was well below 52 per cent, and the historian of a future generation will be at a loss to explain the favoured treatment of France in the matter of reparations.

It is, indeed, difficult to see any essential difference between the expenditure of the French Government on the reconstruction of damaged areas and the expenditure of the British Government on ammunition, etc., for the British as well as the Allied armies. The result was in both cases an enormous increase in the public debt. Had reparations been divided according to the extent of the respective financial sacrifices of the Allies, France's share would have been undoubtedly much smaller, and Great Britain's much larger. Unfortunately, in 1920, when the percentages of the participations of the Allied countries were fixed at Spa, sentimental considerations and the literal interpretation of President Wilson's principles brought a solution which was largely responsible for the financial difficulties of Europe since the war. Germany was obviously incapable of paying the amounts she was forced to undertake to pay, and by insisting upon the payment of amounts beyond Germany's capacity, France was placed in a position effectively to prevent her economic recovery. The French reparations policy bore its first fruits in 1923, when it brought about a complete collapse of the mark. This, however, clearly exceeded the aims of Paris, as it threatened to kill the goose that was to lay the golden eggs. From 1924 onwards, therefore, the effect of the French reparations policy was less spectacular. But it was not less destructive, for, while outwardly monetary stability was maintained, the necessity of finding sums in excess of Germany's current resources gradually undermined the resisting capacity of the reichsmark and brought into being an extremely unsound international monetary situation.

It was evident that Germany had to borrow abroad in order to pay reparations. It was equally evident that she could not go on borrowing indefinitely, and that her excessive external indebtedness was bound to lead to a crisis as soon as some of her creditors attempted to recover their money or even to stop further lending. The French reparations policy was based, therefore, on the assumption that Germany, compelled by the necessity of finding funds for reparations payments to contract a huge external short-term indebtedness, would be bound to become extremely vulnerable; and, consequently, she would not be able to risk arousing the opposition of France, as strained diplomatic relations and the threat of a conflict would mean for her a sudden withdrawal of foreign credits, which again would jeopardise her financial stability. Thus, by opposing a reduction of her reparations claims to a figure which was within Germany's capacity to pay, France put herself in a position to enforce the Treaty of Versailles to the same extent as if she had been given the right to occupy vital points in Germany with military forces. In fact she was placed in a position to claim political concessions beyond the limits of the Treaty of Versailles in return for any reduction she might grant in the amount of her reparations claims.

Reparations were regarded in Paris from two different points of view. On the one hand, they provided a valuable source of revenue, which enabled the Government not merely to pay its own war debts to Great Britain and the United States, but also to redeem part of the debt contracted for the reconstruction of devastated areas. At the same time, they were considered most valuable as a weapon with which both to keep Germany down and to bring pressure to bear upon countries, such as Great Britain, which were working for the restoration of stability in Europe. During the first few post-war years, the financial aspects of reparations overshadowed their political importance. Later on, however, after France had succeeded in balancing her budget, and had wiped out four-fifths of her public debt by devaluating the franc, the comparative significance of reparations as a source of revenue declined and the financial aspects were overshadowed by the political. While, until about 1927, it was of vital importance for France from a financial point of view that Germany's solvency should be maintained, after 1927 France could well afford to make Germany financially insolvent, if that suited her political purpose. Although this would involve the loss of substantial receipts, the simultaneous suspension of war debt payments would reduce her net loss considerably. It was thus no longer of fundamental importance for France to allow Germany to recover to some extent by granting concessions in the matter of reparations. Notwithstanding this, she was reluctant to abandon the financial benefits arising from reparations payments. Naturally enough, she would have preferred a solution by which she could eat her cake and keep it. She desired to weaken Germany financially to a sufficient extent to render her comparatively harmless, and to make her dependent upon French support without rendering her incapable of making any further payments. At the same time, the French policy aimed at weakening the financial power of countries—most of all Great Britain—which were capable of assisting Germany. Although from a financial point of view it would profit France if Germany were enabled, by borrowing in London, New York, and other countries, to continue to pay reparations, the political point of view carried more weight in Paris.

It is often argued from the French side that, far from being aggressive, the French reparations policy was far too conciliatory, and that France repeatedly agreed to the scaling down of Germany's reparation liabilities. But the amount was fixed originally at a figure so fantastically high that France could well afford to make concessions without making any real sacrifice, since she merely gave up what was in any case impossible to obtain. Moreover, the reductions did not in any way curtail France's political power over Germany. Although, in accepting the Young Plan, France agreed as recently as in 1930 to the reduction of her reparations receipts, this did not imply any weakening of her grip on Germany. Even the reduced amount fixed by the Young Plan was safely beyond Germany's capacity to pay, and, besides, as France secured for herself the greater part of the unconditional annuities, the Young Plan actually strengthened rather than weakened her relative position as a reparations creditor.

It will be seen in later chapters that the reluctance of France to agree to President Hoover's proposal for a twelve months' debt holiday in 1931 was largely responsible for the crisis in Central Europe. The uncertainty as to what would be the French attitude after the end of the debt holiday, and what effects it might have, helped to aggravate the crisis. With the weapon of her reparations claims at her disposal, France was in a position to prevent an economic recovery not only in Germany and in Central Europe, but in the world in general.

This weapon was not, however, in itself sufficient to secure a decisive victory for France in the financial combat. It had to be supplemented by another—a "fighting fund" which was to enable France to play an active rôle in the sphere of International Finance. Even from the point of view of the accumulation of this "fighting fund"—which will be dealt with in Chapter V.—reparations policy rendered a useful service. As France was opposed to reparation in kind, she received by far the greater part of her share in the form of cash payments, and these have been an important factor in the accumulation of her gold stock and foreign exchange reserve.

CHAPTER IV

FRANCE'S FINANCIAL RECOVERY

UNTIL 1927 the only weapon France possessed for her financial warfare was her excessive share in German reparations. As we have seen in the previous chapter, it was powerful and was extensively employed. At the same time, however, she was herself on the defensive owing to the weakness of her own financial position, and was unable to play an active part in the sphere of International Finance. In fact, between 1919 and 1926 the franc was exposed to frequent attacks by international speculation, facilitated by an unbalanced budget and by an incessant outflow of French capital. Public opinion in France was inclined to regard these speculative attacks as a retaliation on the part of German and pro-German international financiers to the aggressive use of her weapon of reparations claims. There is nothing, however, to justify this belief. Speculators sold francs because they anticipated a depreciation in its value. It was the same speculators who gambled in mark, lira, Belgian franc, Austrian krone, etc., during the first few post-war years; it was probably the same individuals and firms who directed bear attacks against the peseta from 1927 to 1931, and it was most probably the very same people who speculated against the pound sterling in 1931. International speculation has no nationality and no patriotism: its sole motive is the anticipation of a profit. There is no justification for the theory that there existed any kind of conspiracy between the speculators of various countries in order to accelerate and accentuate the fall of the franc. Frenchmen themselves took a very active part in speculative operations against the franc. A prominent politician with extensive financial interests is said to have speculated against the franc on a very large scale and, according to Paris political gossip, it gave M. Poincaré particular satisfaction to penalise his opponent by squeezing the bears in 1924. Again, in 1925 and 1926, the efforts of M. Caillaux to save the franc were said to have been frustrated by the operations of a prominent French financier who, in subsequent years, played an important part in influencing from behind the scenes the aggressive financial policy adopted by France.

It is true that German banks played a very active part in speculating against the franc, mainly through their affiliates in Amsterdam, but in doing so they merely pursued what they regarded as their business interest. London, like every other foreign exchange centre, was the scene of reckless gambling in francs, but most banks of standing kept aloof from speculative operations of this kind. As for the British authorities, they maintained an attitude of strict neutrality above any suspicion. Admittedly, they did not provide any assistance to the French authorities, but it was, indeed, too much to expect any assistance so long as the French Government had not refunded its war debt to Great Britain; and, in any case, the huge deficit in the French budget would have rendered futile any attempt at stabilisation. The British banking community was ready to assist France on a business basis and, in 1924, it was a credit of £5,000,000 granted by a British banking group, headed by Lazard Brothers and Co., together with an American dollar credit, which enabled M. Poincaré to check the slump of the franc and to bring about a temporary recovery. It is worth emphasising that the British credit was concluded before the American.

Until 1926 the attempts to check the downward movement of the franc failed to produce any lasting results. Apart from the sharp recovery brought about by M. Poincaré's drastic action in 1924, the downward trend was almost uninterrupted. In 1926, however, M. Poincaré succeeded in checking the slump at a moment when it threatened to degenerate into a complete panic such as was experienced in various Central European currencies. He succeeded in arousing, at the eleventh hour, the financial patriotism of the French public, which was at last willing to make the long overdue fiscal sacrifices which were inevitable if the franc was to be placed on a sound basis. The supreme skill with which the operation was planned and carried out deserves the highest possible recognition. We must admit that London and other financial centres which, during the post-war period, grew accustomed to look down upon French finance, have still a few things to learn from Paris. M. Poincaré repeated his tactics of 1924 in squeezing the bears in francs once more during the second half of 1926. This time the attempt had solid foundations, as it was accompanied by a successful effort to place the country's finances in order. Then, before the end of the year, he pegged the exchange in the vicinity of the rate which was subsequently adopted as its definite parity. The choice of the rate of 124 to the pound was, in itself, a master-stroke without parallel in financial history. It was an unpopular choice in the eyes of millions of Frenchmen, as it wiped out four-fifths of the value of *rentes*, bank deposits, and securities with fixed interest. Although in France, as in other countries, a democratic parliamentary system necessitates the adoption of a fiscal policy with an eye to the electorate, M. Poincaré, the greatest financial statesman of our generation, was prepared to face the consequences of his unpopular decision. He realised the immense advantages of stabilising the franc at a level which would enable French producers to undersell their foreign rivals, and through which France could accumulate the huge gold and foreign exchange reserve which was to play a predominant part in International Politics during the subsequent years.

The spectacular financial recovery of France during the second half of 1926 brought about a fundamental change in the balance of power in the domains of International Finance. Until 1927 the two Anglo-Saxon nations virtually monopolised the facilities available for international financial operations. Early in 1927, however, France entered the field as an active power of increasing importance. Human nature being what it is, it is easy to understand the desire of the French authorities and financial circles to take an early opportunity of making their influence felt. For seven years they had been constrained to occupy a subordinate position, and this must have been extremely humiliating for a nation of first-rate political importance. The franc was the plaything of international speculators; foreign centres were unwilling to give help except on humiliating terms. It is only natural that, once France began to feel her feet after the stabilisation of the franc, she should look for an opportunity to assert the return of her financial power. As throughout the crisis of the franc French public opinion put the blame on London for failing to provide adequate assistance and for participating in the bear campaign, it was against London that this demonstration would naturally be directed.

It was inevitable that, in pursuing an ambitious and aggressive policy in the sphere of International Finance, French and British interests should clash. London's financial power had been regarded in France since 1919 as the principal obstacle to the success of the French ambitions for political hegemony on the Continent. The reason why, in the Finance Committee and Council of the League of Nations, the word of the British representatives carried more weight than that of any other nation was that London was in a position to provide financial assistance for those in need of it. Although a great part of the funds raised for reconstruction purposes was actually provided by the United States, the way from Washington and New York to Central and Eastern Europe led through London. The British constructive policy had the full backing of both banking interests and official circles of the United States. So long as this state of affairs existed, France could not hope to become the dictator of Europe. The first step towards that end was thus to weaken London's financial power.

Considerations of a more personal nature also contributed to precipitate a financial conflict between London and Paris. While Mr. Montagu Norman, Governor of the Bank of England, established excellent personal relations with the Federal Reserve system—especially during the lifetime of the late Benjamin Strong, Governor of the Federal Reserve Bank of New York—and with the Governors of most continental central banks, his relations with the French monetary authorities were at best formal, and from time to time they became decidedly strained. French people, with their political mentality, were unable to understand that the constructive British policy of which Mr. Norman was a typical representative was essentially non-political and was not directed against France. They regarded him with hostility and distrust, and credited him with pro-German sentiments. The British policy favouring the reconstruction of ex-enemy countries was attributed in Paris to his influence, and this in itself was a sufficient reason to regard him as an enemy of France. There were, moreover, several circumstances which widened the gap between him and the French monetary authorities. The terms on which, during the war, the Bank of England granted to the Bank of France a credit secured in part by a gold deposit were regarded in France as unduly harsh, and Mr. Norman's unwillingness to revise them was strongly resented. Apart from this, the view was held in French financial and political circles that the Bank of England should have considered it its duty to come to the rescue of the franc. On two occasions, in 1924 and in 1926, the Bank of England was approached, but the terms on which it was prepared to assist were considered unacceptable.

The unwillingness of the Bank of England to give whole-hearted support to the Bank of France was attributed in Paris to the alleged pro-German sentiments of Mr. Montagu Norman. It was said that, while he was always willing to support any of the ex-enemy countries, he was less generous when it was a question of supporting any of the ex-allies, especially France. In reality the Bank of England had perfectly legitimate reasons of a strictly non-political nature for withholding assistance from the Bank of France. The French budget was in a state of confusion, and any artificial stabilisation of the franc would only have increased the difficulty of balancing it. For French fiscal patriotism could only be aroused by the danger of a complete collapse of the franc, and an artificial stabilisation of the currency with the aid of foreign credits would have made it politically impossible for any French Government to carry out unpopular fiscal measures. Moreover, in 1925 it was discovered that the Bank of France, at the instigation of the French Treasury, had been publishing incorrect returns for some time past; the amount of the note circulation published in the weekly returns was well below the actual amount issued. In such circumstances it was not at all surprising that the Bank of England, or indeed any bank, should be unwilling to grant a loan to the Bank of France except on the condition that it was fully secured by gold.

It is to the credit of the French authorities that, rather than accept the terms which they regarded as humiliating, they preferred to forego foreign assistance and work out their own salvation without any external support. Some people are inclined to believe that it was a short-sighted policy on the part of the Bank of England not to adopt a more friendly attitude towards Paris in order to place them under a moral obligation, but it is impossible to say whether such a conciliatory policy would have modified the French attitude in subsequent years. The chances are that it would have made little difference in practice. Gratitude is a rare commodity in the domain of both International Finance and International Politics. The conflict of political interests inevitably led towards a financial clash between France and Great Britain, and this could hardly have been averted completely by more friendly personal relations between the heads of the central banks of the two countries.

The first clash occurred in May 1927. The London money market was startled by the news that the Bank of France had begun to withdraw what were then considered large amounts of gold from the Bank of England. As everybody knew that the French authorities possessed large balances in London, it was felt that these withdrawals might assume considerable dimensions. There was an outcry of protest against these operations in the British Press. At that time the gold standard had not yet been restored in France, and withdrawals of gold on French account were regarded, therefore, as taking unfair advantage of the freedom of the London gold market. Technically, the Bank of France, like every other holder of sterling, was fully entitled to withdraw any amount of gold, and so long as Great Britain was on the gold standard the Bank of England had no right to refuse to sell gold for shipment to France. Morally, nevertheless, these withdrawals were unjustified. The gold standard was established for the benefit of international monetary stability, and the object of restoring the freedom of the London gold market was to meet normal commercial requirements and not the abnormal requirements of the authorities in foreign countries. As a result of the wave of protest aroused by the French action in the Press, and representations made simultaneously by the British authorities in Paris, these operations—which were characterised by contemporary Press criticisms as a "financial Ruhr adventure"—were soon discontinued. At a conference of central banks, held in Washington in August 1927, the Bank of France agreed not to make any purchases of gold, either from the Bank of England or in the open market, without the consent of the Bank of England. The principle that no central bank should withdraw gold from another central bank except with the latter's consent has been adopted as a basis for the co-operation between central banks. The conciliatory attitude of the French authorities was generally attributed to the influence of M. Rist, late Deputy-Governor of the Bank of France, and M. Pouyanne, late Financial Attaché to the French Embassy in London. Unfortunately, both these men relinquished their official posts shortly afterwards.

Thus the first clash between France and Great Britain in the domain of International Finance ended in an agreement which, at the time, appeared to be satisfactory. Subsequent events have proved, however, that this agreement was not a peace treaty but merely an armistice, and that, even without violating its letter, there was ample scope for disregarding its spirit.

CHAPTER V

ORIGIN OF FRANCE'S GOLD STOCK

WE have seen in the last chapter that, although in 1926 the franc appeared to be on the verge of a complete collapse, in 1927, within rather less than a year, France was in a position to make her financial power felt abroad. This fundamental change was the result of the accumulation of a substantial foreign exchange reserve—the nucleus of the huge "fighting fund" which was to become the principal weapon of French Financial Diplomacy, and which was to make History within a few years.

The origin and spectacular increase of France's gold hoard and foreign balances is a complete mystery to the man in the street; it has perplexed even many financial experts. In reality, however, there is nothing mysterious about the process. It is of considerable importance to eliminate any doubt as to the factors that led to the accumulation of this reserve. The French contention is that it was the natural result of the hard work and thrift of the French nation, and that it constitutes, therefore, the legitimate share of the world's gold supply which France is morally entitled to accumulate and to hold. In reality, however, the moral basis of France's gold hoard is open to criticism.

French thrift and industry, admirable as they are, had actually no share in the accumulation of the gold and foreign exchange reserve. Its origin may be traced to the following sources:

(1) Repatriation of French capital which took flight abroad during the inflation period.
(2) France's profit on foreign holdings of francs.
(3) France's excessive share in German reparations payments.
(4) Repudiation by France of four-fifths of her external liabilities in francs.
(5) Unduly generous terms on which the French war debt to Great Britain and the United States was funded.
(6) Artificial export surplus through the stabilisation of the franc at an unduly low level.
(7) Sterilisation of the gold hoard, so as to prevent it from producing its normal effect, which would tend to check the inflow.

(1) We have seen in the previous chapter that the depreciation of the franc between 1919 and 1926 was largely due to the flight of French capital. Notwithstanding all restrictions upon the export of capital—these have proved to be ineffective in every country where they have been imposed—there was a steady outflow of funds to Switzerland, Holland, Great Britain, and the United States. Doubtless this movement accentuated the fall of the franc, and was one of the main causes of France's difficulties; it laid, however, the foundations of the country's immense financial power. It was largely the repatriation of these funds which enabled the Bank of France to accumulate a huge gold holding and foreign exchange reserve. Whether those responsible for the management of the financial

policy of France had this object in view in allowing the franc to drift as far as it did, it is difficult to say. Any financial statesman of vision must have realised that the efflux of capital was a blessing in disguise, as it provided a potential source of strength for the future. From a moral point of view, however, the process was not a creditable one. Whatever its ultimate result, it was brought about through the disloyalty of many thousands of French citizens, who, in the pursuit of their own interests, circumvented the law and increased the difficulties of their country in a time of crisis. Thus, the origin of the gold accumulated through the repatriation of these funds was not to be found in thrift and industry, but in disloyalty and lack of confidence in the national currency.

(2) While the greater part of the exports of French capital was carried out while the franc was between 50 and 100 to the pound, the bulk of this capital was repatriated at a time when the rate was between 124 and 250. France thus repurchased the francs which she sold to foreigners who trusted her at about half the price she obtained for them originally. As the amount involved ran into milliards of francs, the net profit was by no means negligible and contributed to no slight extent to the accumulation of the gold and foreign exchange reserves. It can hardly be claimed that this part of the gold stock was accumulated through thrift and hard work, and that France is morally entitled to withhold it from the rest of the world.

(3) As we pointed out in Chapter III., the French share in reparations was in excess of her relative share in the costs of the war. It is true that she was nominally entitled to it on the basis of the damages which she

suffered through the German invasion. But it is necessary to recall the fact that, soon after the war, Germany offered to reconstruct with her own workmen the devastated areas of France. This offer was rejected, as France preferred to receive cash payments, no matter how much inconvenience the transfer of those payments might cause to the rest of the world. These payments, which contributed to the increase of the French gold stock, represented in part German thrift and industry, and in part funds lent to Germany by British, American, and other investors and banks. They can hardly be claimed, therefore, to represent French thrift and industry.

(4) The stabilisation of the franc at 124 wiped out four-fifths of France's external indebtedness in terms of francs. The case of the French *rentes* issued in London during the war is the best-known example, but there are others besides. The French balance of payments has been improved by this act of repudiation, which was thus in part responsible for the accumulation of the French gold reserve. It is difficult to see how this portion of the gold stock could possibly be attributed to French thrift and industry.

(5) France funded her war debts to Great Britain and the United States at a time when, owing to the depreciation of the franc, her financial situation was regarded with undue pessimism. For this reason, both British and American Governments were highly generous, and agreed to a reduction in the amount entirely unwarranted by France's inherent economic resources. The ratification of the agreements was delayed until 1928, when France had recovered her financial strength, and it was obvious that the reductions were granted in misleading circumstances. It was thanks to these un-

warranted reductions that French receipts from reparations exceeded war debt payments. They have contributed to the improvement of France's balance of payments, and have been responsible for part of the accumulation of her gold reserve. French thrift and industry could hardly account for the amount involved.

(6) In 1926, when the franc was stabilised, the index number of French wholesale prices was 620, corresponding to a gold index number of 124. At the same time, the wholesale index number for Great Britain was 145 and for the United States 148. Thus, at the moment of the *de facto* stabilisation, the French wholesale price level was, roughly speaking, 20 per cent below the world price level. This naturally tended to encourage exports and discourage imports, and it made France a cheap country for foreign visitors and residents. As a result of these influences, the French trade balance produced year after year a surplus of visible and invisible exports over visible and invisible imports, and the amount of gold accumulated as a direct effect of the stabilisation of the exchange below its economic level is considerable. Its influx could be attributed to M. Poincaré's financial master-stroke rather than to French thrift and industry.

(7) Although there was a tendency towards the adjustment of French prices to the world level, for nearly five years the French authorities were successful in resisting it and in maintaining a discrepancy in favour of France by means of preventing the influx of gold from producing its normal effect upon prices. It was not until 1931, when the world price level declined to the level of prices in France, that this difference was eliminated. Had the influx of gold been allowed to take

its natural course, the working of normal economic tendencies would have soon checked the excessive accumulation. A considerable part of the gold stock was acquired through artificial interference with the working of economic laws. French industry and thrift can hardly claim the credit for this.

It is obvious from these considerations that the accumulation of the "fighting fund" was a largely artificial process, and that its details were such as to dispose entirely of the French claim to have a moral right to withhold the surplus from the rest of mankind.

The accumulation of the "fighting fund" was encouraged by the French authorities by every possible means. To accelerate the process, M. Poincaré left the world in a state of uncertainty for about eighteen months as to the definite rate of stabilisation of the franc, and made no announcement of his decision until June of 1928. Everybody expected him to follow the example of Signor Mussolini, who, for considerations of prestige, brought about an appreciation of the lira to a high level, where its stabilisation became a difficult task. It was widely believed that M. Poincaré would be unable to resist the pressure, brought to bear upon him by the army of rentiers and by the political parties on whose support his parliamentary existence depended, to raise further the value of the franc. It was anticipated that the pegging of the franc at 124 was only a respite in its upward movement. Although the number of those who anticipated the restoration of the franc to its pre-war parity was small, there was a predominant belief, both in France and abroad, that the definite rate of stabilisation would be somewhere between 75 and 100. As a result, French capitalists, who during the period of inflation exported their savings, hastened to repatriate their funds so as to take advantage of the appreciation of the franc. Had M. Poincaré stabilised the franc legally at the end of 1926 or the beginning of 1927, as he was advised to do from many quarters, the process of the repatriation of French capital would have been a very slow one. Once the franc was legally stabilised, there was no inducement for the repatriation of these funds, especially as, in order to make the stabilisation successful, taxation had to be raised and maintained at a high level. Thus, had M. Poincaré stabilised the franc legally soon after he attained the level at which he intended to maintain it, the repatriation of French capital would have spread over a number of years; the bulk of it would not have returned until after the reduction of direct taxation which took place several years later. As it was, the greater part of the French funds which took refuge abroad was returned to France during the eighteen months ended June 1928 in the hope that the benefit arising from a further appreciation of the franc would provide ample compensation for the high level of taxation.

The accumulation of the "fighting fund" brought about by this movement during the period of pre-stabilisation was accentuated by an influx of foreign funds. Foreign speculators, assuming that the appreciation of the franc would continue, transferred large amounts to Paris, notwithstanding the low interest rates prevailing in that centre. For some time in 1927 this plethora of foreign funds caused an *embarras de richesse*, but, in spite of this, the movement was helpful, as it assisted in the consolidation of the franc. It is true that after the legal stabilisation of the franc, foreign speculators withdrew their funds, but this outflow did not materially weaken the monetary position of France. It was amply covered by the export surplus which was the result of the stabilisation of the franc below its economic parity.

CHAPTER VI

GOLD IN INTERNATIONAL POLITICS

THE employment of gold movements in the service of foreign policy has the appearance of an innovation. It is, indeed, new in the sphere of gold arbitrage, though it is not new to politics. Some centuries ago international gold transactions of a certain kind, undertaken for political motives, played a considerable part in shaping History. On frequent occasions gold found its way between one country to another from the exchequers of allied or hostile Governments into the private purses of those capable of influencing the foreign policy of their countries. But for some of these gold transactions the outcome of some of the wars of the eighteenth century would probably have been different, and History might possibly have taken quite another course.

In our day gold seems once more to have won prominence in International Politics, although its uses have altered. Changed conditions necessitate new methods, though the new and more sophisticated manœuvres of our own age may be inspired by the same Machiavellian spirit as the primitive devices of days gone by. The shipment of gold no longer serves the purpose of bribing influential personalities to betray their countries, at least not in the world of Western civilisation. The modern practice is to use it as a means of affecting the monetary situation of the countries in question in such a way as to induce their Governments to change their foreign policy. It is also used to tempt Governments which stand in urgent need of external assistance to sell the independence of their foreign policy in order to save their countries from financial disaster. Both these methods have been extensively applied by the French Financial Diplomacy during the last few years. It is the former with which we are concerned in the present chapter.

Although the French authorities have strictly observed the letter of the Washington agreement of 1927, and have refrained from taking the initiative in direct withdrawals of gold, in practice the agreement has made but little difference. So long as France was not on a gold standard it was, of course, impossible for her to withdraw any gold from London otherwise than through direct purchases by the Bank of France. In June 1928, however, France restored the gold standard, and from that time onwards the Bank of France was in a position to attract gold without having to make itself directly responsible for its purchase. The central bank of any country on a gold basis is always in a position to increase its gold reserve by maintaining the Bank Rate at a comparatively high figure, or by bringing about an appreciation of its exchange through the sale of part of its foreign currency reserve. For the latter operation the Bank of France was particularly favourably placed, for, possessing huge sterling and dollar balances, it was able to manipulate the exchanges in order to attract gold. Moreover, the French Treasury and the Caisse d'Amortissement controlled huge funds, the administration of which could influence the situation in the French money market, and could indirectly influence French banks to withdraw funds from abroad.

Thus, even without making any direct purchases abroad, the French authorities were in ·a position to attract huge amounts of gold to Paris. Indeed, they took every opportunity to increase their holdings at the expense of other centres, especially of London. To some extent the inflow was a natural consequence of the substantial favourable trade balance. But the export surplus could hardly be considered as a normal economic factor, as it was largely due to the choice of an unnaturally low level for the stabilisation of the franc. By applying a self-imposed restriction, according to which the Bank of France was not to increase further its foreign exchange reserve, the export surplus was bound to find its way back to France in the form of gold so long as Paris abstained from lending abroad. The financial statesmen of France duly realised the advantages of possessing a large gold reserve beyond the immediate financial requirements of the country. They foresaw that sooner or later this gold stock would play a decisive rôle in European politics. They were also aware that they could secure political advantages, not merely through the possession of a huge gold stock, but also through the manner of its accumulation. The surplus demand for francs was bound to result in an influx of gold; the task of the authorities confined itself to regulating when and whence the gold should come.

The simplest solution for everybody concerned, from a financial point of view, would have been to repatriate the surplus in 1928 and 1929 by shipments from New York. At that time the American authorities would have welcomed a reduction of their gold stock, as it might have checked in time the Wall Street boom. The gold withdrawn from New York would not have been missed, and the transaction would not have affected adversely international monetary stability. It is true that, owing to the high rate of the dollar, it was at that time more profitable to import gold from Great Britain or Germany. But the difference was a negligible amount, and the repatriation of the surplus without causing any inconvenience by such a huge abnormal transaction would have certainly been worth a moderate sacrifice. Other central banks, less wealthy than the Bank of France—such as the Bank of Poland and the Czechoslovak National Bank—repeatedly purchased gold in New York when it would have been more profitable for them to meet their requirements in London.

It is reasonable to assume that considerations of a business nature would not, in themselves, have prevented the French authorities from choosing this solution also. It must have appeared to them, however, undesirable, for considerations of a political nature, to repatriate the surplus by withdrawals of gold from New York. It is true that the possession of a huge gold stock would have represented the same power whether the gold came from the United States or from other countries. But this solution would have deprived French Financial Diplomacy of one of its most powerful weapons. The process of withdrawing gold from New York would not have carried any political advantages at that time, because New York did not object to losing some of its surplus. It was not until September 1931 that her turn came to be subject to French gold withdrawals of a political nature. In 1929 it was politically advantageous that the gold influx should come from London and Berlin rather than from New York.

From the restoration of the gold standard in France in June 1928 until the suspension of the gold standard in Great Britain in September 1931, France imported from London gold to the amount of £136,000,000, the predominant part of which was withdrawn from the Bank of England. The flow of gold to France was by no means continuous. Whenever relations between France and Great Britain became strained, the franc moved against sterling and there were heavy withdrawals of gold from London through normal commercial transactions. Whenever there was a tendency towards political *rapprochement*, the gold efflux subsided.

The first serious attempt to influence British external policy by means of gold withdrawals was made in 1929 on the occasion of the Hague Conference in August and September. Throughout the year London had lost much gold as a result of the drain of funds to Wall Street. In spite of repeated increases in the Bank Rate there was a continuous pressure against sterling, and the Bank of England's reserve declined below the figure of £150,000,000 indicated by the Cunliffe Report as the minimum normal requirement. Soon after the victory of the Labour Party at the general election in May 1929 the French gold withdrawals began to assume considerable dimensions. In June Mr. Snowden's statement that he would press the claims of British holders of French *rentes* provoked retaliations in the form of heavy gold withdrawals to Paris. During the Hague Conference the firm stand taken by Mr. Snowden against the unjustified reduction of the British share in reparations receipts

E

resulted in further heavy gold withdrawals. It may be said that his uncomplimentary remarks concerning M. Chéron, the French Minister of Finance, cost the Bank of England the loss of some £20,000,000 of gold.

Towards the end of 1929 and early in 1930 gold withdrawals came to a standstill as a result of the better understanding between the British and French Treasuries, which led to the definite adoption of the Young Plan at the second Hague Conference in January 1930. The withdrawals were resumed, however, in May, when negotiations for the mobilisation of German reparation annuities once again caused a clash between British and French interests. The rigid opposition of the British Treasury to the issue in London of an amount of the German Reparations Loan exceeding the British participation in its proceeds was regarded in Paris as an act aiming at sabotaging the plan of mobilising German reparations. The aim of the French policy was to mobilise the largest possible amount of German unconditional annuities and to place the largest possible amount of these mobilised annuities in countries other than France. The main object of this policy was to provide a further means of increasing the French "fighting fund". As the predominant part of the unconditional annuities was allotted to France by the Hague Agreement, the mobilisation of these annuities tended to increase French balances in the centres where the Reparations bonds were placed. The British monetary authorities duly realised the disadvantages of this course, and hence came their opposition to the issue of a large amount of the Young Loan in London. At the same time they also opposed the French proposition that all Reparations bonds should be made interchangeable, as this might have prepared the way for the dumping of the French holding of Reparations bonds on the London market.

The attitude of the British Treasury in opposing a solution which would have further increased French balances in London was justified by simple considerations of self-defence. The disadvantages of being exposed to heavy French withdrawals were duly realised by that time, and the insistence of the French authorities upon a solution which, if adopted, would tend to increase the inconveniences of London threw some light upon the aims of their policy. It was in itself sufficient to dispose of the favourite argument of the apologists for the French gold policy, that the French authorities were anxious to avoid causing any inconvenience to London, but that they were powerless against natural economic tendencies.

As the British Treasury refused to yield, France eventually had to agree that the proceeds of the London issue of the Young Loan should be retained in England, and that the London issue should not be interchangeable with the remainder of the loan. This minor victory for British Financial Diplomacy was soon followed by French reprisals in the form of a renewal of heavy withdrawals of gold during May and June 1930. After a comparatively short interval, the withdrawals were resumed once more in the autumn and winter of 1930. But this time they were not due to any direct political motives. Owing to a threatening bank crisis in France the French banks were anxious to repatriate part of their sterling balances in order to increase their liquidity. Although the French authorities would have been well in a position to stop the movement by converting part of their dollar balances into sterling, they refrained from doing so as it was convenient for them to have the British gold reserve reduced. In August and September the Bank of England's reserve rose above £160,000,000, leaving an ample safety margin over and above the minimum requirements. This was not a desirable state of affairs from a French point of view, as it weakened their power to bring pressure to bear upon Great Britain at an opportune moment. For this reason, the withdrawal of gold, although not encouraged, was definitely welcome to the French authorities.

In December 1930 the French Government unofficially sounded the British Treasury as to whether it would be prepared to arrange a meeting in order to establish co-operation for the purpose of checking the gold outflow. It was apparently felt in Paris that, owing to the possibility of an early German demand for the revision of the Young Plan, it would be desirable to secure more friendly relations with Great Britain. A series of meetings took place between British and French Treasury officials in London and Paris. At the first of these meetings the British Treasury officials produced a chart showing that the outflow of gold from London to Paris almost invariably coincided with an increase in French official balances with the Bank of France. The obvious conclusion was that it was the manipulation of these balances which regulated the flow of gold, and that the French Treasury was, therefore, well in a position to check the movement, should it wish to do so, by refraining from any sudden reductions of the French market's resources. In reply the French Treasury experts produced at the next meeting a chart showing that the outflow of gold was a natural consequence of the fluctuation of interest rates in London and Paris. Their contention was that, whenever the margin between money rates in the two centres declined, it ceased to be profitable for French banks to maintain balances in London; hence the wholesale repatriation of funds, which was responsible for the withdrawal of gold. In their opinion, the British authorities were well in a position to check the outflow by raising the Bank rate to a sufficiently high level to make it worth while for French interests to maintain large balances in London. From a French point of view this attitude is easily understandable. As the Bank of France, the French Treasury, and the Caisse d'Amortissement had at that time at least £100,000,000 in London, a difference of 1 per cent in the Bank rate meant an additional yield of £1,000,000 per annum. From a British point of view, however, it appeared anything but desirable to raise the Bank rate at a time when the country was suffering from acute trade depression. In any case, the French argument that it was the margin between the interest rates in London and Paris that regulated gold movements did not dispose of the British argument that the operations of the French Treasury in the Paris money market had a good deal to do with the French gold withdrawals. After all, these operations had a predominant influence on interest rates and on the resources of the money market in Paris, and in many cases they were responsible for the contraction of the margin between rates in London and Paris.

The French Treasury eventually agreed to regulate its operations, as far as it was possible to do so without detriment to its own interests, in such a way as to cause London the least possible inconvenience. The Bank of France agreed to waive its refusal to accept bar gold of standard fineness, which caused much inconvenience to London during the second half of 1930, and which was responsible for a depreciation of sterling below gold export point. As a result of these arrangements, towards the middle of January the outflow of gold actually ceased, and was not resumed until the beginning of the German crisis.

It has often been stated that the attitude of the French authorities towards gold movements was that of strict neutrality. Whenever it was suggested that the depreciation of sterling was due to the withdrawal of French official balances, these statements were always emphatically denied from Paris. There is no possible means of checking the accuracy either of the suggestions or the denials. The French Bank return gives only the total amount of the foreign exchange holding without specifying the amount held in any particular currency. The first attempt that was made early in 1931 by the Macmillan Committee to ascertain the amount of French balances in London was frustrated by the refusal of the London branches of French banks to comply with its request to supply particulars as to their holdings of sterling bills. By allowing their bills to run out, or by selling them in the discount market, the French authorities were always in a position to withdraw funds from London without actually reducing their bank balances and deposits. It is known that during the second half of 1930, and throughout 1931, the Bank of France reduced its foreign bill holdings and increased its foreign balances. It is impossible to state, however, how its total holdings of sterling were affected by these operations. On the other hand, it is known in well-informed circles that during 1930 the French Treasury reduced its London balances to a comparatively negligible figure. While, during previous years, it held in London a substantial amount so as to provide for war debt payments, not only to Great Britain but also to the United States, after the establishment of the Bank for International Settlements this was considered no longer necessary. Possibly the liquidation of the French Treasury's holdings of sterling contributed directly or indirectly to the weakness of the exchange during 1930.

According to the apologists for France's gold policy, the withdrawal of gold from London to Paris was a natural and inevitable result of the French export surplus and the reluctance of the French public to take up foreign loans. Even if we were to admit that the French authorities and banking interests had no means of re-lending the export surplus and thereby checking the accumulation of gold, this argument does not dispose of the theory that gold movements were engineered for political purposes. Had the exchanges been left to take care of themselves, gold movements would probably have followed a seasonal trend in accordance with normal trade tendencies. In actual fact, however, as we have seen above, they coincided almost invariably with political differences. This provides strong circumstantial evidence that between 1929 and 1931 the French authorities made extensive use of the weapon of gold withdrawals in pursuing a political end. It is impossible to supply concrete proof of the theory that the authorities themselves, through their foreign exchange operations, were directly responsible for the depreciation of sterling whenever an efflux of gold from London suited their political purposes. Their operations—which were in any case covered by the secrecy to which all banks are pledged concerning their clients

—were extremely complicated, and were carried out through dozens of channels, so that nobody except those conducting them could ascertain whether, at any time, they were on balance buyers or sellers of sterling. But even if we were to admit that the operations of the French authorities in the foreign exchange market, as well as in the French money market, were strictly non-political, this would not dispose of the possibility that the operations of other French banks were influenced by the authorities for political purposes. It is a widely known fact that French banks usually obey the wishes of their Government even if it is not in accordance with the interests of their shareholders or their clients. They are willing to issue a political loan despite their conviction that it is a bad investment and that the transaction may be detrimental to their goodwill. They certainly would not hesitate to take a hint from the authorities to withdraw their funds from London at a moment when in doing so they could assist the external policy of their country. It is, of course, possible to imagine that French holders of balances in London divined every time the moment when it was their patriotic duty to provoke gold withdrawals by selling their sterling, even without having to be specially instructed by the authorities.

One thing is certain. Even if we were ready to give the French authorities the full benefit of the doubt concerning their "neutrality" towards the fluctuations of sterling and the withdrawals of gold, this does not exonerate them from the blame for having omitted to prevent the movement which was bound to undermine London's international financial position. The usual answer to this charge is either that they were not in a position to help, or that, after all, France is not an institution of public charity, and that there was no reason why she should help unless it appeared desirable from her own point of view. As to the first answer, it is based upon certain technical restrictions imposed upon the operations of the Bank of France by its antiquated statutes and by its agreement with the French Treasury. For the most part, these technical obstacles were a matter of interpretation, and could easily have been overcome with a little goodwill. As to the second, the claim that it was not the moral duty of the French authorities to do everything in their power to prevent or counteract any inconvenience caused to Great Britain by French holders of sterling, it can hardly be upheld in face of the fact that the post-war financial troubles of Great Britain were due to the support, both financial and military, which she gave to France between 1914 and 1918.

The negotiations between the British and French Treasuries in January 1931 were not the only attempt to reconcile the conflicting interests of the two countries. There were several French financial experts who viewed the widening of the breach with growing concern, and who were anxious to improve financial relations between London and Paris. M. Henri Pouyanne, while French Financial Attaché in London, made several successful attempts to bring about a better understanding between the British and French financial authorities. Even after he resigned his post to take up a banking appointment, he assumed the rôle of an unofficial intermediary on one or two occasions with the object of restoring more amiable relations. His successor, M. Rueff, is also known to have made efforts to establish better understanding between the financial interests of both countries. M. Germain Martin, who was Finance Minister in M. Tardieu's Cabinet in 1930, was another of these moderate and enlightened Frenchmen, and it was largely thanks to his influence that the *rapprochement* of 1930 was initiated. Unfortunately, owing to the change of Government, M. Germain Martin relinquished his post, and his successor pursued a less conciliatory policy. The change in the personnel of the Bank of France at the end of 1930 was also detrimental to any attempt at *rapprochement*. M. Moreau, who is said to hold comparatively moderate views, resigned the Governorship of the Bank in October 1930, and was succeeded by M. Clément Moret, who was credited with being less accommodating than his predecessor. A much more important change was the appointment of M. Farnier as Deputy Governor of the Bank of France. Before he took up this post, he occupied a high position in the French Treasury, and is believed to have been largely responsible for the aggressive policy which M. Moreau, possibly often against his own better judgment, was obliged to pursue. The strength of ultra-nationalistic influence in the Bank of France was probably in part responsible for the accentuation of the conflict between that institution and the Bank of England which culminated in a deadlock in July 1931 and was one of the causes of the financial crisis.

CHAPTER VII

FIGHT FOR SUPREMACY

LONDON's financial strength was the chief obstacle to the French ambitions of becoming the financial dictators of Europe. French Financial Diplomacy set itself, therefore, the task of eliminating this obstacle by strengthening Paris and by weakening London. Withdrawals of gold were not the only means to that end. The fight was carried on in every sphere of International Finance. It was fully realised in Paris that the liquid resources amassed since 1926 could be used for political as well as financial ends much more advantageously if Paris were to possess a technical organisation similar to that of London. Steps were taken, therefore, to improve the facilities of the Paris market. The measures taken to achieve that end and their results are described in detail in the author's book *The Fight for Financial Supremacy* (Macmillan, 1931). Here we shall confine ourselves to indicating the connection between those endeavours and the main object of the French financial warfare.

Although the possession of an international banking business carries with it certain financial advantages, they would not have been, in themselves, a sufficient inducement for France to concentrate considerable efforts upon the scheme. The French Financial General Staff was aware, however, that, in order to obtain the maximum of political advantage out of its "fighting fund", it had to be handled skilfully, and to that end the technical organisation of the Paris market had to be improved. Steps were taken, therefore, to create a bill market in Paris. It was realised that London's superiority was due, to a great extent, to her excellent discount market, and it was hoped that, if Paris could capture part of London's discount business, this would deal a severe blow to London's position, which had already been weakened since the war by the development of the discount market in New York. Arrangements were made for providing acceptance credit facilities through the existing banks as well as through the creation of a new bank specialising in acceptance business, the Banque Française d'Acceptation.

While the destructive spirit that inspired France's gold policy is open to criticism, nobody could raise objections to the constructive endeavours aiming at the development of Paris as an international financial centre. After all, a great nation with ample financial resources at her disposal is entitled to create facilities for better technical administration of her funds. Even if the progress of Paris were to be detrimental to London's position, British interests would not have had a legitimate grievance on that account. Possibly, if France's ambitious policy had been successful in a constructive direction, the destructive part of her policy might have been abandoned. Had Paris succeeded in rivalling London as a financial centre, she might have regarded it as no longer necessary to attempt to undermine London's strength. However, the attempt to establish a discount market in Paris proved a failure. In the absence of adequate experience and old-established connections, Paris was unable to obtain the right type of business. The acceptance credits granted by French banks to German banks at the outset resulted in a plethora of German finance bills. The high proportion of German bills to the total volume of bills in the Paris market was regarded with displeasure by the authorities, and, early in 1929, steps were taken to discourage lending to Germany. The Bank of France raised the rediscount rate for German and other Central European bills to $\frac{1}{2}$ per cent above the official Bank rate, and, at the same time, it was intimated to French banks that excessive lending to Germany was viewed with disfavour. French banks, which have always been subject to political influence, took the hint, and during the following two years credits to Germany were reduced to a negligible figure. They were unable to replace the business thus lost, and the Paris discount market, after an active start, experienced a prolonged period of stagnation and decline.

The attempt to establish an international market for long-term loans proved equally unsuccessful, mainly as a result of political influences. Although the authorities endeavoured to assist in the development of the Paris capital market by removing the prohibitive fiscal charges upon new issues, at the same time they expected this market to serve political purposes without regard for normal financial considerations. The only loans which were admitted to Paris were those of the political allies of France: Poland, Jugoslavia, and Roumania. The French investing public, which had had such a disastrous experience with politically inspired Russian loans, distrusted these new ventures in political finance, and the response to the issues was unsatisfactory. As a result, the French financial houses, which were already immobilised by the undigested part of the French portion of the Young Loan, had to shoulder the burden of these political loans in addition. This rendered them incapable of expanding their activity further, although the complete stoppage of international loan business in both London and New York provided them with an excellent opportunity of acquiring a *clientèle*. Negotiations were carried on in various directions, but, apart from the political loans mentioned above, no substantial transactions materialised.

The establishment of the Bank for International Settlements provided another avenue through which French Financial Diplomacy hoped to weaken London's influence. From the very beginning, France was determined to prevent at all costs the choice of London as the seat of the Bank. In spite of the technical superiority of London, which would have provided the Bank with better facilities for development, it was decided to establish the Bank at Basle. British interests reluctantly agreed to this, although it was obviously a defeat. They hoped that, no matter where the Bank was situated, it would provide a highly valuable means for co-operation between Central Banks and would lead to a better financial understanding between nations. The French conception of the Bank was, however, an entirely different one. It was hoped in Paris that the Bank would come entirely under French influence and that it would become the instrument of French foreign policy. They were encouraged in their hopes by the fact that the Bank of France was in a position to provide a substantial part of the Bank's financial resources. As, from considerations of domestic politics, the Federal Reserve system was constrained to keep almost entirely aloof from the Bank, and the Bank of England was beginning to feel the persistent pressure of French withdrawals from London, French interests hoped to attain a practical monopoly of its management. They succeeded in obtaining the appointment of M. Pierre Quesnay to the post of General Manager. Although, in ultra-nationalistic French quarters, M. Quesnay has been suspected of harbouring international sentiments, these suspicions are unjustified, as he has rendered extremely valuable services to French Financial Diplomacy.

As the British interests concerned with the Bank agreed that it should be located in Switzerland, they might have succeeded in obtaining in return the appointment of a British General Manager had they persisted in such a demand. Possibly the importance of the Bank was underestimated in London, or it may have been expected that British interests could be adequately safeguarded by the representatives of the Bank of England on the Board of Directors. To some extent this latter assumption was correct, but, considering that there was only one Board meeting every month and that, consequently, the management had to be allowed a comparatively free hand, this state of affairs led to frequent frictions between board and management. On various occasions when M. Quesnay took the initiative, the majority of the directors were not altogether pleased with the *fait accompli* with which they were confronted. Hence the stormy Board meetings, which were anything but beneficial from the point of view of co-operation between Central Banks. The French directors, who invariably supported the action of the General Manager, were often left in a minority, but on several occasions the Board could not see its way to amending the decision.

On more than one occasion the Bank's action was decidedly detrimental to British interests. The case of the Yugoslavian stabilisation scheme provides a characteristic example. For some years, a British and a French group had been competing for the Yugoslav stabilisation loan. Negotiations with the British group had reached an advanced stage, but, owing to adverse conditions in the international bond market, the issue had to be postponed time after time. To meet the Government's most urgent requirements, the British group granted a short-term credit in 1929. A year later, however, following M. Quesnay's visit to Belgrade, it was announced that the negotiations with the British group had been abandoned and that the Bank for International Settlements had granted a credit to Yugoslavia. A little later, the stabilisation loan was definitely concluded with the French banking group.

Thanks to the firm stand adopted by the British directors, and to the support they often received from other non-French directors, the French plan of making use of the Bank for the purposes of France's external policy was not always successful. To overcome this obstacle to their ambition, French interests endeavoured to obtain additional support on the Board by the appointment of a number of new directors. At the Board meeting of April 1931, they proposed to appoint representatives of the Jugoslav, Czechoslovak, Polish, etc., Central Banks, so as to assure in future a majority on the Board. Their proposal was, however, rejected, and the only new appointments were those of the representatives of three "neutral" countries: Sweden,

Switzerland, and Holland. The Bank for International Settlements proved, therefore, on the whole, a disappointment from the point of view of French political ambitions. Although to some extent it may have weakened London's international financial position, the damage was not substantial. It was presumably realised in Paris that neither the Bank nor the development of Paris as a financial centre provided sufficiently strong weapons, and that the only way in which France could have her will in the sphere of political finance was by continuing her direct attacks upon London's financial strength and stability. An opportunity for this soon arose as a result of the financial crisis in Central Europe.

CHAPTER VIII

FRANCE AND THE WORLD CRISIS

EVER since a considerable number of countries restored the gold standard, the world has been suffering from an acute scarcity of the metal. As the United States retained the gold she hoarded during and after the war, and other countries, such as Spain and the Argentine, were also reluctant to part with their surplus, the remaining gold stock available for monetary purposes was not sufficient to meet the increased requirements of all the countries on a gold basis. Most central banks wanted more gold than before the war, not merely because the price level and the note circulation were considerably higher, but also because, owing to unsettled economic and financial conditions, everybody considered it desirable to hold a substantial margin above the minimum prescribed by law. The output of new gold was not sufficient to meet the increased requirements, which could have been really satisfied only by a redistribution of the surplus gold held in the United States and in a few other countries. It was obvious that unless this happened within a reasonable time, the scarcity of gold supplies was bound to lead to a readjustment of prices in a downward direction.

Until about 1928 there was a distinct tendency towards the redistribution of the gold stock of the United States, thanks to the liberal lending policy of the New

York banks. As a result of the Wall Street boom, however, this movement suffered a set-back. At the same time, France appeared on the scenes as a buyer of gold on a large scale. While at first her purchases attracted comparatively little attention, before very long the world realised that it was confronted with a tendency which was likely to be the source of immense trouble.

The question of the extent to which the French policy of gold hoarding has been responsible for the world economic crisis has been the subject of heated controversy. According to an extreme school, the maldistribution of gold, brought about by the French hoarding policy, was solely responsible for the decline in world prices, which again was the principal cause of the world-wide depression. Even if we cannot accept this extreme theory, there is no doubt at all that the French gold policy had a large share in the responsibility for the economic troubles from which the world has been suffering during the past two years. The apologists for the French gold policy (or, as they like to put it, "the absence of a gold policy" on the part of France) maintain that it is impossible to trace any connection between the maldistribution of gold and the falling tendency of world prices. They point out that there was no deflationary tendency during 1929 or 1930 which could be regarded as responsible for the decline. Even if it were impossible to prove statistically the direct connection between French gold purchases and the slump in commodity prices, the existence of such a connection can safely be taken for granted, in accordance with the generally accepted theories of price movements. Undoubtedly, there have been a number of individual causes responsible for the fall of prices in every individual group of commodities, but the existence of these factors does not dispose of the theory that the general downward trend was mainly due to the monetary factor. After all, the monetary factor always works through the intermediary of factors affecting particular groups of commodities. When there is monetary inflation or deflation in a country, prices do not rise or fall simultaneously and to the same extent, and there are always people who seek to explain the fall in the prices of certain commodities by the conditions prevailing in the local market. The arguments of those who wish to exonerate the monetary factor from the blame for the fall in world prices from 1929–1931 are not convincing, any more than are the arguments of those who, during the war, denied that the rise in prices was mainly due to monetary influences.

In 1929 the international monetary situation became particularly vulnerable, owing to the flow of funds to Wall Street from every centre. In order to check this flow, the Bank of England, and most continental central banks, had to raise their Bank rates repeatedly. While they were struggling against this drain, France was engaged in increasing her gold hoard, considerably beyond her requirements. She withdrew large amounts both from Great Britain and Germany, thereby accentuating the upward trend of interest rates. It is a commonplace of economic text-books that higher interest rates tend to force merchants and manufacturers to liquidate their commodity stocks, and tend, therefore, to bring about a downward tendency of prices. There is no reason to suppose that the experience of 1929 was an exception to this rule.

It is a general habit to regard the Wall Street slump of November 1929 as the starting-point of the world economic crisis; as a matter of fact, the slump itself was merely the consequence of the alarming symptoms which tended to create pessimism among speculators. The most important of these symptoms was unquestionably the falling tendency of wholesale prices, brought about by the increase in Bank rates some months previous to the Wall Street collapse.

In all fairness, France should not be held responsible for the Wall Street slump, which would have taken place sooner or later in any case. Had the boom continued for another few months, the reaction would have been all the more violent. Had the French gold hoarding policy come to an end in 1929, France could have claimed with justice that she had rendered the world a valuable service in contributing towards checking the reckless gamble which was heading towards disaster.

Unfortunately, France's appetite for gold did not subside after 1929. She continued to withdraw huge amounts from London and other centres during 1930 and 1931, at a time when the world was suffering from an acute economic depression owing to the declining tendency of the international price level. Instead of co-operating with other leading central banks in the task of checking the downward trend of prices, France accentuated the evil by sterilising large amounts of gold. Admittedly, she was not the only country guilty of this practice. The United States had also increased her gold holding almost continuously throughout the period of economic depression, mainly out of the supplies of Latin America and the Far East. But while, in the case of the United States, the inflow of gold was merely due to the absence of any defensive measures against the current, in the case of France it was the result of a deliberate policy which began with the stabilisation of the franc at an unjustifiably low level and continued throughout the crisis.

For a long time France remained comparatively immune from the repercussions of the world-wide economic depression. This was due to a number of special circumstances. In the first place, France stabilised her currency below its economic value, and her price level was considerably below the world level. Thus, while the price level was falling in many countries, it was practically steady, with a slight upward trend, in France. It was not until the fall in world prices eliminated the discrepancy between the price level in France and that in other countries that French prices began to decline in accordance with the international tendency. Another reason for the comparative immunity of France from the world depression was the fact that she was more self-sufficient than most other countries. Moreover, thanks to the work provided by the reconstruction of her devastated areas, her industries were able to accumulate substantial reserves, and the crisis found them in a sound position. In France, the devaluation of the franc to one-fifth of its pre-war parity also contributed to increase the resisting capacity of her productive elements. While in Germany and in some countries of Central and Eastern Europe, excessive inflation wiped out the working capital of producers, in France inflation was checked in good time to prevent it from producing such an effect. In its early stages, inflation tends to be beneficial to producers as it enables them to repay their debt in depreciated currency. It is only in its advanced stages that inflation becomes dangerous to producers and consumers alike. As France succeeded in stopping at the right moment, her industries and agriculture had all the benefit of the depreciation of the currency—at the expense of the rentier, of course—without any of its disadvantages. French producers were thus better equipped to face the depression than producers in most other countries.

These circumstances explain in part why France was reluctant to respond to the overtures made to her for closer international co-operation in the matter of her gold policy. The French nation was comparatively happy, and the increase in the gold stock of the Bank of France was regarded with pride and satisfaction. As was the case in the United States during the years that preceded the slump, the increase in the gold stock came to be regarded as an indicator of growing prosperity. Press and public opinion alike began to realise that the gold that was accumulating in the vaults of the Bank of France represented political power. Although few people, if any, outside the Financial General Staff of France, had any idea in what way the possession of surplus gold stock could be converted into political advantage, it was generally felt that sooner or later the gold would provide a useful support for France's foreign policy. In such circumstances, any agreement on the part of the French authorities to collaborate in the redistribution of gold, or even to check the inflow, would have been most unpopular and would have met with violent opposition in Parliament. When, in 1930, in reply to the French argument that the statutes of the Bank of France preclude the French authorities from taking measures to check the influx of gold, it was pointed out that these statutes could be changed by legislation, the idea was rejected as impracticable; no French Government would have dared to face the unpopularity of introducing such legislative measures.

Had France been subject to the influences of the international depression to the same extent as other countries, possibly she might have been more inclined to adopt a policy of genuine co-operation. This is, however, by no means certain. In France, Government, Parliament, Press, and public opinion are governed by political rather than economic considerations, and it seems probable that the average Frenchman would have been willing to suffer economic disadvantages for the sake of the glory of political power represented by a huge gold stock. In any case it is doubtful whether French politicians, economists, and journalists would ever have allowed the public to realise that their economic troubles were caused by the accumulation of gold.

Had it been possible to come to an understanding towards the end of 1930, or even at the beginning of 1931, for a reasonable redistribution of the world's gold supply, the depression would have come to an end before it assumed catastrophic dimensions. Unfortunately, every attempt to induce France to adopt a policy of co-operation failed. The Bank for International Settlements proved incapable of achieving much in this direction; nor did the lengthy discussions of the Gold Committee of the League of Nations lead to any material results. France continued to accumulate gold, world prices continued to decline, and mankind continued to suffer increasingly from economic depression.

Apart from the material effect of withholding gold supplies from their natural employment, the French gold policy affected the international situation also through its psychological influence. The feeling that, in face of the most severe economic crisis in modern

History, the monetary authorities of the leading countries were engaged in a conflict instead of co-operating for the common good, tended to increase uneasiness and distrust. It was not a mere coincidence that, when at the beginning of 1931 France showed herself to be inclined to adopt a more friendly attitude, there was a distinct improvement in the international economic situation. Prices ceased to fall, and the tendency pointed towards a slow recovery. This improvement would have undoubtedly continued but for the unfortunate Austro-German Customs Union scheme, the appearance of which once more aroused ultra-nationalistic sentiments in France and put an end to the conciliatory tendencies of her international financial policy.

Admittedly, France had every reason to distrust and oppose the Austro-German Customs Union scheme as a first step towards a political union between the two nations. It is difficult to find an excuse for the aggressive policy of Germany in jeopardising the peace of Europe with this scheme at a time when France showed some inclination to adopt a conciliatory attitude. Germany's ambition to play once more an active part in International Politics was, undoubtedly, the direct cause of the accentuation of the world economic crisis in the spring of 1931. The clumsy and provocative way in which the scheme was presented was rightly resented in France. The admission of this fact, however, does not exonerate France from the blame for opposing the German policy by the use of financial weapons which brought about an international financial disaster. As the ruling of the Hague International Court proved, it would have been possible to prevent the Union without making use of such destructive weapons. In any case, Germany would have been willing to drop the scheme in return for a reasonable revision of the Young Plan. If France wanted Germany to go beyond the letter of the Peace Treaty she could have induced her to do so by relinquishing, in return, part of her rights arising from the Treaty. Instead of this, France resorted to force—not in a military, but in a financial sense.

The unfavourable change in the international political atmosphere caused by the conflict over the Austro-German Customs Union scheme resulted in a set-back in the international economic situation. The recovery in commodity prices and stock prices that took place during the first quarter of 1931 was soon wiped out in the revival of pessimism brought about by the gathering of clouds on the political horizon. France can hardly be blamed alone for this; it is only natural that she should oppose a policy tending to imperil her security. If her opposition to the scheme resulted in strained international relations, it was largely the fault of those who initiated the scheme. Had France awaited with patience the ruling of the Hague Court or the result of the impending direct negotiations between various Governments, she would have been exonerated from responsibility for bringing about the financial collapse. Unfortunately, French politicians were unable to exercise such self-restraint. They put themselves in the wrong by taking the first opportunity of striking at their opponents with the weapon of their financial power, without caring whether, in doing so, they dealt a fatal blow to the world's financial structure.

CHAPTER IX

THE CREDITANSTALT AFFAIR

UNTIL the Spring of 1931 the evolution of the world crisis was slow and gradual. From May, however, events began to develop with dramatic rapidity. The Creditanstalt *débâcle* became the starting-point of a banking crisis without precedent in Central Europe, which again developed within a few months into an international monetary crisis comparable only to the post-war currency chaos. It was the Creditanstalt troubles which gave rise to the first open encounter between British and French interests in the battlefield of International Finance. Until then the fight was carried on behind the closed doors of Treasuries, central banks, and conference rooms. The general public was unaware of the financial struggle, and those concerned in it either denied its very existence or remained silent. In June 1931, however, a violent clash occurred between British and French interests, with world-wide publicity, and the pretence of friendly co-operation had to be discarded.

On May 11 the Austrian Government announced that, owing to heavy losses suffered by the Creditanstalt, it had become necessary to reconstruct the bank with the assistance of the Government, the National Bank, and the Vienna house of Rothschild. This announcement came to the banking world like a bolt from the blue. Although it was generally known that the Creditanstalt, like most other banks on the Continent, was largely immobilised, it was taken for granted that, owing to its excellent connections, the bank would be able to pull through without any open reconstruction. Its name had been for generations a household word for solid and sound banking, and, on account of its reputation and its close association with the Vienna house of Rothschild, it enjoyed first-class credit in the leading financial centres. During the last two years it had made extensive use of the credit facilities which were offered freely by foreign banks, so that at the time of the crisis its foreign liabilities amounted to some £15,000,000. It was hoped that the reconstruction scheme, which provided for considerable additional capital, would be sufficient to allay any fears. Undoubtedly, from a technical point of view, the bank's position was improved by the writing down of its losses; but those who believed that this would be sufficient to maintain confidence reckoned without the psychological factor. The Austrian depositors, with the memory of a number of bank failures since the war still fresh in their minds, lost their heads, and there were steady withdrawals of local deposits. Foreign creditors, alarmed by these withdrawals and by the delay in the granting of a definite guarantee by the Austrian Government, began to call in credits.

At the same time unexpected difficulties delayed the issue of 150,000,000 schillings of Austrian Treasury bonds for providing funds for covering the Austrian Government's share in the deficit of the Creditanstalt. While in May the French authorities promised to participate in the transaction, they postponed a definite agreement, and on June 17 they presented the

Austrian Government with an ultimatum stating that the only condition under which France would participate in the loan would be that the Austrian Government should abandon the German Customs Union scheme. This move created great indignation not only in Austria and Germany, but also in Great Britain and the United States. It was regarded as an open attempt at political blackmail not only against Austria, but against all countries interested in the reconstruction of the Creditanstalt. The indignation was all the more justified since the price offered by France for a political concession of vital importance was negligible. France was prepared to take over a short-term loan of some £2,300,000, and in return for this she demanded that Austria should sacrifice her political independence—it was a demand that she should sell her birthright for a mess of pottage.

The crisis of the Creditanstalt has made it plain that, in her present form, Austria is incapable of continuing her existence as an independent economic unit. The most natural solution for Austria, both from a political and an economic standpoint, would be absorption in Germany. This is, of course, obviously contrary to French interests, as a Germany with a population of over 70,000,000 would be a source of permanent menace to France with her population of about 40,000,000. It was thus to the interest of France that Austria should be kept apart from Germany, even at the cost of financial sacrifices. Apart from France, and possibly Czechoslovakia, no other country had any interest in keeping Austria and Germany apart. It was, therefore, hardly reasonable to expect countries such as Great Britain or the United States to make big financial sacrifices in order to continue to maintain Austria in her present form for the exclusive convenience of France. If France desired to keep Austria and Germany apart, it was she who ought to have provided the major part of the means for securing a reasonable existence for Austria. The argument that the United States of Europe scheme would provide Austria with an adequate compensation for abandoning the Customs Union with Germany was hardly convincing, for there is no likelihood of establishing a European Customs Union in the lifetime of the present generation. As it was to the interest of France that the Customs Union scheme should be dropped, it was obviously her duty to provide an immediate solution by taking over the bulk of a substantial long-term loan, which would have given Austria another chance to consolidate her economic position. Had France offered a long-term loan of, say, £20,000,000 to Austria in compensation for the abandonment of the Customs Union scheme, the offer would have been considered a fair one; but she wanted to attain the maximum result with the minimum sacrifice. It was well known in Paris that the success of the reconstruction of the Creditanstalt depended upon the placing of the 150,000,000 schillings of Austrian Treasury bonds, and that the solvency of Austria depended on the reconstruction of the Creditanstalt. It was also assumed that, without French participation, it would be impossible to place the Austrian Treasury bonds at a moment's notice. London had her own difficulties, and was not in a mood for assisting others any further than was absolutely necessary. Assistance from New York was out of the question owing to the unfavourable situation in Wall Street and the unwillingness of American banking to increase commitments in Central Europe. The smaller continental financial centres could not be expected to provide much assistance without the co-operation of one of the leading centres. There was no hope for any further assistance from the House of Rothschild, beyond the amount already granted. The London house helped the Vienna house as far as possible, but the Paris house had to refrain from assisting its Austrian cousin, as such action would have crossed the aims of the French Government. France hoped, therefore, that Austria would be forced by these circumstances to accept the French terms. There was, indeed, no time for hesitation. The demand was presented at the eleventh hour, so as to leave no time for Austria to look round for an alternative solution.

The Austrian Government was, however, unwilling to yield to pressure. Rather than submit to such political blackmail, it was prepared to abandon the attempt to reconstruct the Creditanstalt, even if it meant insolvency for the country. To safeguard the interests of Austria's creditors, as well as of Austria herself, the Bank of England stepped in at this stage and undertook to provide the whole amount of £5,000,000 required by the Austrian Government. The situation was thus saved, for the moment at any rate, and a definite agreement between the creditors and the Austrian Government was soon concluded.

The Bank of England's action provoked a wave of indignation in France. It was regarded as a political manœuvre in support of the Customs Union scheme. As a matter of fact, the Customs Union scheme was not viewed with favour in London, and the motives of the Bank of England in providing support for the Austrian Government were purely financial. As we said above, the Austrian Government was, in any case, determined not to pay the price which France demanded for her support; so that, even if the Bank of England had kept aloof, France would not have attained her end. The object of the Bank of England's action was to safeguard the interests of the British creditors of the Creditanstalt by enabling the Austrian Government to carry out the reconstruction of that institution. It was, moreover, obvious that a collapse of the Creditanstalt would lead to an international financial disaster, and the Bank of England considered it its duty to prevent it even at the cost of heavy sacrifice, and at the risk of displeasing French interests. Thus there is no need to look for political motives to explain the Bank of England's action. It is characteristic, however, of French mentality to judge others by themselves and to suspect political motives behind everything. As France herself would never have undertaken such constructive action without any direct political benefit being attached to it, French official circles and public opinion took it for granted that British action was prompted by similar motives. The result was a strong resentment, which accentuated the tension between the two countries and rendered relations between the Bank of England and the Bank of France more strained than ever. French Financial Diplomacy felt the defeat very keenly, and looked forward to the day which should bring it its opportunity to retaliate.

With the exception of France, the Bank of England's action was applauded all over the world. It constituted a moral victory of first-rate importance, as it disclosed to the world the sharp contrast between the constructive British financial policy and the destructive French political finance. It is true that the material results of the victory were short-lived. As will be seen in later chapters, the subsequent unfavourable developments in the position of London compelled the Bank of England in September to ask for the repayment of the loan; and Austria was eventually forced to submit to the dictation of France as regards the Customs Union scheme. While in June such capitulation was regarded as unthinkable, three months later it did not surprise anybody. During those three months, considerations of pride and prestige faded into the background in face of the rapidly growing danger of a complete economic collapse. Austria was not the first country, nor the last, to yield to French pressure. The British assistance was unable to prevent the ultimate victory of French Financial Diplomacy. In spite of this, the moral effects of the British victory of June were not eradicated by the French victory of September. When History has to pronounce judgment on the events of these days, the facts of the Anglo-French duel over Austria will throw into strong relief the contrast between the constructive British policy and the narrow destructive policy pursued by France.

CHAPTER X

THE GERMAN CRISIS

THE immense significance of the Creditanstalt crisis was not realised at first. Hardly anybody suspected that it would become the starting-point of the greatest financial crisis in history. Even in well-informed banking circles it was hoped that the difficulties would be overcome, and that the situation would remain substantially the same as it was before the fateful announcement of May 11. Within a few weeks, however, it became evident that the harm done by the Creditanstalt affair was irreparable, and that its effects would be felt far beyond the borders of Austria, or even those of Central Europe. The immediate consequence of the crisis was that the United States, in its disappointment at the Creditanstalt disclosures, was filled with a strong distrust of Central Europe in general. Up to the moment of the announcement of its reconstruction, nobody had suspected that there was anything wrong with the bank, in spite of the fact that its difficulties were not altogether of recent origin. Bankers had, therefore, good reason to ask whom they could trust, if, even in dealing with first-class banks, they were exposed to such unpleasant surprises.

Until May 11, American banks lent freely to the leading Central European banks, especially to the big

German banks. They were by no means alone in this. The "D" banks and a few other German and Central European banks commanded absolute confidence in London just as they did in New York, Amsterdam, or Switzerland. Their credit facilities in the leading financial centres were almost unlimited, and they made extensive use of them. While, until 1928, German borrowing abroad mainly assumed the form of long-term loans, from 1929 the Wall Street boom and the subsequent slump made the issue of external loans impossible. As Germany was compelled to pay reparations far in excess of the surplus of her trade balance, the only way in which she could raise the funds without upsetting the stability of her exchange was by encouraging short-term borrowing abroad. The Reichsbank had to maintain a comparatively high Bank rate so as to attract foreign short-term funds, though, thanks to the high standing of German banks, a comparatively moderate discrepancy between money rates in Germany and abroad was sufficient to induce foreign banks to lend to Germany. It is important to emphasise that, but for these short-term credits, Germany would have been compelled to suspend reparations payments in 1928 or 1929. In this way the country which derived most benefit from these credits was France, being the principal recipient of German reparations. Yet French banks participated only to a very small extent in the short-term lending to Germany. Until the spring of 1929 they were willing lenders, but under official influence they began to curtail their loans to Germany in April 1929, and by the time of the crisis their participation was negligible. In consequence, the German banks were compelled to draw upon the facilities offered in London, New York,

Amsterdam, and Switzerland to fill the gap created by the withdrawal of French credits.

Although there were at the time no statistical data available as to the extent of German short-term borrowing in various foreign centres, many bankers were beginning to feel that they had committed themselves too heavily in Germany and Central Europe. If, in spite of this, few of them, if any, considered it desirable previous to May 1931 to reduce German credits, it was because of the sharp competition in the field of International Banking. While, before the war, London was the only acceptance market in the world, since the war, rival acceptance markets had developed in New York, Paris, Amsterdam, and Switzerland. At the same time, commercial banks which, before the war, took very little interest in acceptance business, had begun, since the war, to take a keen interest in this branch of banking activity. As the volume of sound business did not grow in accordance with the increase of facilities offered, bankers were reluctant to refuse any apparently sound proposition, and were inclined to overlook the basic principle that no bank should commit itself too heavily in any one country. Bankers in Great Britain and in other lending countries have been subject to much criticism for the extent to which they committed themselves in Germany; but it is easy to be wise after the event. Until the Creditanstalt crisis, there appeared to be no reason to regard loans to first-class German banks as unsound. Apart altogether from the merits of the borrowing banks themselves, the lending banks had every right to take it for granted that, in case of trouble, the German Government would support them to the utmost rather than permit them to fail. Subsequent events proved this assumption justified, for the big German banks of international standing which got into difficulties received from their Government all the assistance that they required.

The only point in which banks are open to criticism is that they did not reckon with the political factor. Although they realised that Germany would not be able to pay reparations for ever, they took it for granted that the scaling down of reparations would be a comparatively smooth process. This assumption appeared to be reasonable on the ground that, since the Ruhr adventure, France had shown herself willing to agree to revisions of her reparations claims. The figures of the Dawes Plan constituted a substantial reduction as compared with the previous amounts, while the Young Plan again went still further in the way of adjusting reparations claims to realities. It appeared from the experiences of the period 1924–1930 that politicians always managed to come to some kind of compromise, even though occasionally their conferences were threatened with a breakdown. This explains why bankers assumed that politicians would not do anything to disorganise the international financial situation.

Doubtless, this assumption would have been justified but for the fact that by 1931 France felt herself strong enough financially to embark upon an aggressive policy. As a result of the accumulation of a huge fighting fund in her gold reserve and foreign exchange reserve, and in view of the adverse conditions which were paralysing the financial strength of London, her Financial General Staff felt that the moment had arrived for making a bid for financial dictatorship over Europe. In the past, it had been in France's interests to avoid a financial crisis in Germany which would have jeopardised her reparations claims. In 1931, however, she was in a sufficiently strong position to be able to afford to forego reparations in order to secure political advantages. Moreover, while in previous years the strength of London and New York would have made it impossible for France to attain her end, in 1931 both these centres were weakened considerably by the world economic crisis, and they had to struggle with their own financial problems. Thus, the assumption that politicians could not afford to provoke an international financial crisis, although justified until 1930, was vitiated in 1931. Bankers are not altogether to blame for having failed to foresee this change. Most people, even the usually well-informed international bankers, were completely in the dark as to the sinister plans of French Financial Diplomacy. To have reckoned with this factor would have required an exceptional foresight. Even when international relations between France and Germany became strained owing to the Customs Union scheme, it was taken for granted in banking circles that this controversy would take its normal course and that, after a series of conferences, a compromise would eventually be reached.

In May 1931, however, American banks began to call in their credits from Germany on an ever-increasing scale. Their change of attitude was due mainly to their disappointment over the Creditanstalt affair. The delay in the definite agreement on the reconstruction scheme for the Creditanstalt was fatal, and the Austrian authorities bear a large share of the responsibility for the accentuation of the wave of distrust against Central Europe. While they were discussing legal technicalities, the drain of American funds went on. American banks did not possess sufficient experience in International Banking, or adequate banking traditions, to realise that their policy might produce fatal effects upon their debtors and that it was, therefore, against their own interests suddenly to curtail credit facilities. British, Swiss, and Dutch banks attempted for a while to play the game, but, owing to the increasing withdrawals of funds by American banks, they felt compelled to take steps to protect their own interests. As a result, throughout May and June, the withdrawals of foreign funds from Germany continued unabated, and the Reichsbank had to part with huge amounts of gold to maintain the stability of the reichsmark. The Franco-British clash over the Creditanstalt provided a belated warning of the gathering storm and precipitated the outward flow of funds.

It was at this stage that President Hoover made his historic proposal of one year's moratorium for reparations and war debts. It was a gesture which proved that the policy of the United States was inspired by the same constructive spirit as that of Great Britain. It was criticised in some quarters on the grounds that it came too late or that it was inadequate. Indeed, the moratorium of twelve months merely increased uncertainty as to the situation after the end of this short period. Had it been granted for a longer period, it might have induced bankers to leave their funds in Germany. As it was, it failed to check the outward flow because everybody wanted to be clear of Germany before the end of the twelve months. But, in spite of this, the merits of the proposal were incontestable. At a time when the United States was suffering from a severe economic crisis and when her budget had a huge deficit, the sacrifice of one year's annuities from Europe merited high praise. The gesture raised the moral standing of the United States as a creditor beyond measure. Those who, in the past, were inclined to censure her for her attitude to war debts, were compelled by Mr. Hoover's proposal to revise their critical view. Even if the actual relief provided by the plan was not sufficient, it ought to be appreciated as the first departure from the rigid attitude which the United States has always adopted in the matter. Moreover, it was reasonable to assume that this first step would be followed by a complete revision of the existing agreements.

Unfortunately, the reception of the plan in France damped hopes in this respect. While, in practically every country, the plan was greeted with enthusiasm, in France it was received with suspicion and misgiving. French official circles were fully aware that a drastic revision of war debts would deprive France of one of the most powerful weapons in her financial armoury. In the face of world opinion, France could not afford openly to frustrate the plan, but, in delaying its adoption by petty haggling over details, she succeeded in reducing to a minimum its beneficial psychological effect. While at the moment of the announcement of Mr. Hoover's proposal, it was hoped that this might be a preliminary to a complete cancellation of war debts and reparations, the attitude of France made the world realise that, even if the United States could be induced to make this enormous sacrifice, there was no ground for expecting a conciliatory attitude on the French side. As a result of the delay in the adoption of the Hoover Plan, the withdrawals of foreign funds from Germany and the flight of German capital continued unabated and, by the time the proposal was adopted by France, the crisis had reached a state when it could no longer be checked.

The support which the Reichsbank received from the Bank for International Settlements, the Bank of England, Federal Reserve banks, and the Bank of France was unable to stop the avalanche for more than a few weeks. The short-term credit was soon exhausted, and neither the Bank for International Settlements nor the Bank of England nor the Federal Reserve banks were in a position to grant further assistance. It became evident that France was the only country which was in a position to save Germany from financial collapse.

The dreams of French financial statesmen had thus come true. The financial stability of Germany was in the hands of France, and she was in a position to dictate her terms. France was willing to help—at a price. She was willing to provide the funds required to avert the threatening banking crisis if the German Government was prepared to drop the Customs Union scheme and to abandon the construction of a new cruiser. Unfortunately, it was politically impossible for the German Government to accept these terms. Had it agreed to what Nationalist newspapers termed a "second Treaty of Versailles", it would have been swept away by a Nationalist revolution. Thus, whether or not the French demand was, from the French point of view, justified, it was impracticable.

One of the reasons why international bankers had trusted Germany implicitly in the past was that they relied upon the sober and realistic mentality of the Germans, politicians and public alike. Nobody believed that a situation might arise when, rather than agree to political concessions, Germany would choose financial default as the alternative. It was the unexpected that happened. Rather than obtain French assistance at the price of abandoning the Customs Union and the cruiser (both of which had to be abandoned eventually in any case) Germany stopped the payment of her external short-term credits. This act has done irreparable harm to Germany's reputation as a debtor, and it will take more than a generation to live it down. And this means that in future, even if conditions become normal, Germany will no longer be in a position to borrow extensively in order to pay reparations. In withholding her assistance, France has thus lost her chances of obtaining reparations beyond the amount of the actual export surplus of Germany. Her victory was thus an expensive one. She could have attained the same result at a much slighter cost if, instead of making use of the weapon of her financial power, she had sought to come to terms with Germany on a reasonable basis. Had France been willing to consent to a reduction of reparations as the price for these political concessions instead of insisting upon the politically impracticable demand of linking financial support with the abandonment of the Customs Union and the cruiser, part of her reparations claims could have been saved. As it is, the likelihood of France ever receiving any further substantial reparations payments from Germany has vanished, and she will eventually have to consent to a much more substantial reduction of her reparations claims than would have sufficed in June 1931 to induce Germany to accept her terms.

CHAPTER XI

THE CLIMAX IN CENTRAL EUROPE

THE Central European crisis was rapidly approaching its climax during the first half of July. Hopes that, as on previous occasions, common sense would eventually prevail and a solution be found at the eleventh hour, were rapidly vanishing. It was becoming more and more evident that this time the crash was inevitable. While on previous occasions, all that was expected of France was that she should abandon part of her claims, which were, in any case, impossible to realise, on this occasion she was expected to grant actual financial assistance to save the situation. As it was obvious that Germany was not prepared to pay the price demanded for French assistance, the chances of an eleventh-hour solution were negligible. Hence the increasing anxiety of foreign banks to recover their funds from Germany and the growing flight of German capital. It was obvious that the Reichsbank would be unable to stand the strain much longer.

At this time several important failures occurred in Germany in which both foreign and German banks were involved to a considerable extent. The most notorious of these failures was that of the Nordwolle, the circumstances of which were such as to inspire strong distrust. As the Darmstädter und National-bank was heavily involved in this failure, depositors began to withdraw their funds, and the position of the bank became critical. An attempt was made to save it, but it failed owing to the inadequate co-operation between German banks. As a result the bank—which was the second largest in Germany—suspended payments on July 13. The German authorities had to take elaborate precautionary measures to prevent a panic. All banks were ordered to remain closed, and when, after two days, they eventually re-opened they were placed under restrictions as to the amount they were entitled to pay out to any individual customer. Although no official moratorium was declared, in practice an almost complete moratorium was established by the measures taken. This was the only alternative to a collapse of the reichsmark through a depreciation of the exchange caused by the withdrawal of foreign funds and through internal inflation caused by the necessity of meeting a run by local depositors.

It may well be asked if the suspension of the Darmstädter und Nationalbank was really inevitable. As the Government had, in any case, undertaken to guarantee its liabilities, and as it was re-opened subsequently under the same restrictions as those operating for other German banks, its suspension appears to have been superfluous. Possibly it was meant to be a gesture to indicate the gravity of the German situation. In any case, however, restrictions upon payments abroad would have been inevitable even if the Darmstädter und Nationalbank had not closed its doors.

The German banking crisis produced tremendous repercussions in every part of the world. Its immediate consequence was the suspension of a number of banks in Central Europe, the Baltic States, and the Near East. The country which was most affected was

Hungary. For two months past a banking crisis had been developing in Hungary, owing to the distrust of Central Europe brought about by the Creditanstalt crisis. As the Hungarian General Credit Bank of Budapest was closely associated with the Creditanstalt, it was taken for granted that the latter's difficulties would affect the former, and on this supposition there were heavy withdrawals of local deposits and foreign credits. As in the case of Austria and Germany, France was willing to help at the price of political concessions but the Hungarian Government hoped to obtain support from other quarters; about this more will be said in a later chapter. The Hungarian Government was compelled to follow the German example in imposing restrictions upon payments by banks, more especially as regards their external liabilities. Similar restrictions were introduced in Danzig, Latvia, and other countries. The reason why Austria remained comparatively immune from this crisis was that she had weathered her own storm in May and June and that the two years' standstill agreement with the foreign creditors of the Creditanstalt had, to some extent, consolidated her position. In a way it had been a blessing in disguise to get into trouble at an early stage of the crisis, when creditors could afford to grant liberal terms.

France was the only country to remain unaffected by the German crisis. As we have already observed, French banks called in their funds from Germany in 1929 and 1930, and their commitments were negligible. This was not due to the superior skill or instinct of French banks, but to political influences. While in the past financial interests in France had often been sacrificed for the sake of political interests, on this occasion the political factor proved extremely helpful. It may be said that the French banks, in calling in their German credits in 1930, when it was still possible to do so, did the right thing for the wrong motive.

All over the world, creditor countries such as the United States, Great Britain, Holland, and Switzerland, whose interests in Germany were considerable, suffered a heavy blow through the German crisis. In the United States it aggravated the depression and weakened the position of banks to no slight extent. Some of the leading American banks were involved with amazingly large amounts in spite of their efforts during the previous few months to reduce their commitments. As, however, the Federal Reserve Banks were in a very strong position and the amounts of German commitments, large as they were, represented only a small fraction of total American banking resources, the German crisis did not cause any immediate concern as to the banking situation in that country. Great Britain was in a less fortunate position. Although her participation in German credits was much smaller than that of the United States, the comparative weakness of the Bank of England's gold position and the extent to which individual banking houses were committed gave rise to a feeling of uneasiness abroad as to the possible repercussions of the German crisis on the London market. It is stated that, on the occasion of his Paris visit in July, Mr. Arthur Henderson, then Secretary of State for Foreign Affairs, told M. Laval that in case of a collapse of Germany there would have to be a moratorium in Great Britain. Although these reports were emphatically denied, they certainly gave rise to anxiety in Paris, and French banks began to withdraw their balances. The exchanges moved against us and gold was withdrawn from the

Bank of England on an unprecedented scale. Switzerland and Holland also had their share of troubles through the repercussions of the German crisis. The former was affected to a particularly great extent owing to the large amount of German capital in Switzerland and the equally large amount of Swiss credits to Germany. Although, in theory, these two items practically offset each other, in practice those Germans who had funds with Swiss banks were by no means identical with those who borrowed from Switzerland, and an early attempt to offset German claims by counter-claims had to be discontinued. There were several bank failures in Switzerland, and there were runs on a number of banks, which had to be supported by other institutions. In spite of the extremely strong position of the National Bank, the Swiss situation was regarded with some concern. The same was true, though in a lesser degree, of Holland. Her position was complicated by the fact that a number of German banks possessed affiliates in Amsterdam, which had acquired considerable influence. Owing to the general state of uncertainty, banks in Holland, Switzerland, and other centres sought to increase their liquidity by withdrawing funds from London, and this again aggravated London's position.

The only countries which remained comparatively immune from the banking crisis for a while were France and her political allies. Although difficulties in Austria and Germany led to a run on various Czechoslovakian, Roumanian, Polish, and Yugoslav banks, the run was resisted without much difficulty, either by means of actual support from France or else because the mere anticipation of such support was sufficient to restore confidence. It was widely realised that France was now in a position to distribute rewards to her allies, at the same time as she was able to inflict punishments upon her rivals and opponents. Roumania was the only country among her political allies which suffered to some extent through the repercussions of Central European banking crises. Several of her banks suspended payment. Apparently the French support to Roumania was somewhat half-hearted, presumably because the friendly attitude of the new regime towards Germany was viewed with disfavour in Paris. Thus, while France was willing to prevent a severe crisis in Roumania, she did not go so far with her support as in the case of other allied countries.

Throughout July and August, conference followed conference in an effort to find a solution to the German crisis. It was hoped against hope that France might be induced to agree to assist Germany, especially as it was becoming daily more evident that the German crisis was jeopardising international financial stability. Conference followed conference in Basle, Paris, and London. The bankers, who were asked by the politicians to find a solution, handed back the task to the politicians on the ground that the German problem had ceased to be financial and that the solution lay with the politicians. The latter again, being unable to agree on anything essential, referred the task back to the bankers. The hopes of an understanding were frustrated by the negative result of the London conference, at which the French representatives vetoed discussion of any question essential to the solution of the crisis.

Admittedly, Germany shared with France the responsibility for the deadlock. When France reluctantly agreed to the Hoover Moratorium, it was reasonable to expect that Germany would reciprocate the gesture in some form, possibly through a suspension of her naval plans and of the Customs Union scheme during the period of the moratorium; but no such gesture was forthcoming. This explains to a great extent why France based her attitude towards the German crisis upon the principle of "give and take". She was prepared to come to the rescue of Germany, provided that the latter would agree to drop the Customs Union scheme and to abandon the construction of a new cruiser. But Germany refused to yield. Her attitude was subject to much criticism in every part of the world, but, at the same time, it must be admitted that the internal political situation made it impossible for the German Government to adopt any other attitude. Had it agreed to the French demands, most probably it would have been overthrown by the extreme Nationalists; and this would have been against the interests of France as well as those of the creditors of Germany. While Germany cannot be exonerated from blame for the crisis, her unbending attitude was largely due to the aggressive policy pursued by France ever since the war.

In spite of the immense difficulties she had had to cope with, Germany stood the strain of the financial crisis remarkably well. Her population remained calm notwithstanding the hardships imposed upon it. The stability of the exchange was maintained in July and August, at the cost of stopping the payment of external short-term credits. Had the German nation behaved as sensibly in politics as in finance, the crisis would have taken a much milder course and would have come to an end before long. But few nations, if any, can be sensible in the political sphere, and it must be admitted that the aggressive French attitude during

H

the previous twelve years would have tried the patience of a nation of saints. In any case, Germany has earned the admiration of the world for having succeeded in averting a financial collapse, for the time being at any rate, practically without any active external assistance.

CHAPTER XII

LONDON'S CRISIS

WE have seen in the previous chapter that the London Conference of July failed to produce any result. No agreement could be reached for co-operation in measures to overcome the difficulties caused by the German financial crisis. France was unwilling to assist unless Germany was prepared to agree to political concessions. It would, indeed, have been too much to expect her to abandon the fruits of her financial victory at the moment when, after several years of hard work, they were almost within her reach. Admittedly the victory was not complete. Neither Austria nor Germany was yet prepared to yield to French political pressure. The former obtained temporary relief from Great Britain, while the latter was, at that time, still hoping to obtain relief from Great Britain and the United States. Undoubtedly Dr. Brüning must have realised by then that London was not in a position to help, and that New York was unwilling to throw good money after bad, so that the only source from which Germany could expect assistance was Paris. It was, however, politically impossible for him to pay the price demanded by France for financial support. Public opinion in Germany had not realised at that time that London's position was becoming more critical every day, and that, far from being able to assist, she might herself require assistance. So long as it was not generally realised that no assistance could come from Anglo-Saxon sources, no German Government could possibly face the consequences of accepting France's support at the price of abandoning the Austro-German Customs Union and the construction of the new cruiser.

It was obvious that France could not reap the fruits of her financial victory so long as London's plight did not become evident. The next move in the financial warfare was, therefore, to dispel any doubt as to London's difficulties. This end could be achieved in two different ways, either by allowing sterling to collapse under the pressure of withdrawals of French and other foreign balances, or by affording Great Britain assistance at the eleventh hour on conditions which would make London's dependence on Paris obvious. The French authorities chose the second alternative. The collapse of sterling was against their interest, because the Bank of France and the French Treasury held substantial sterling balances, and because it would have affected adversely French foreign trade. This was duly realised in Paris; and, although the foreign policy of France's financial statesmen was guided primarily by political considerations, financial and commercial conditions were not altogether neglected. It was of importance from the point of view of France's external policy that London should be weakened, and that her weakness should become evident, but, if this end could be achieved without paying the price for it in the form of losses on sterling balances and losses in French foreign trade, France would naturally prefer to choose that solution.

At this stage there was indeed no need for any particular efforts on the part of the French authorities to aggravate London's position. As we have seen in Chapter XI., the Central European crisis produced grave repercussions upon the London market. London banks had commitments in Germany amounting to nearly £100,000,000, which had become hopelessly frozen after July 13. The situation was the same as far as London's claims against Austria and Hungary were concerned. It was an open secret that several leading acceptance houses were heavily involved in Central Europe, and rumours as to their alleged difficulties were freely circulated in foreign countries. This was one of the causes of the withdrawal of foreign balances from London. Apart from this, foreign banks holding sterling balances became anxious to increase their liquidity, by withdrawing these balances. In the early stages of the movement the fear of a depreciation of sterling was well in the background. It is only when the outward trend of gold assumes considerable dimensions that foreign banks become seriously concerned about the possibility of a collapse.

The big French banks were among the principal foreign holders of sterling balances, and were taking the lead in French withdrawals. It is estimated that the amount they withdrew from London between the middle of July and the middle of September was between £40,000,000 and £50,000,000. Admittedly there was no trace of withdrawals on the part of the Bank of France and the French authorities. At the same time nothing was done in Paris in the early stages to check this movement, though it was bound to lead to a collapse of sterling. The franc moved strongly against sterling, declining on several occasions well below gold export point. There was a record withdrawal of gold from London to Paris; and although French banks were by no means alone in withdrawing francs, their sales of sterling were by far the heaviest, and were mainly responsible for the embarrassment of the London market. Had the French authorities taken timely steps to counteract the effects of these withdrawals, confidence would have been restored, and the efflux of funds in other directions would have stopped automatically. This course was not, however, in accordance with the aims of French Financial Diplomacy. It was not until the last week of July that the French authorities began to realise the critical position which was being created. The gold reserve of the Bank of England was declining rapidly, and, by the end of July, it was barely above £130,000,000.

At this stage something unexpected happened. Much to their surprise, foreign exchange dealers noticed that during the last week of July the Bank of France had begun to support sterling. It freely purchased any amount of sterling thrown on the market by French banks desirous of withdrawing their balances. At the same time the French Press, which up till a few days previously had been revelling in pessimistic forecasts of sterling's prospects, suddenly changed front, and, with a unanimity that appeared astonishing to anyone not acquainted with the discipline of French newspapers in matters of foreign policy, adopted an attitude of extreme optimism. Apparently the French authorities realised that London had been weakened to a sufficient extent, and that the point had been reached beyond which the safety of their sterling investments was in danger. It was to their interest not to allow things to drift further. Accordingly, the Bank of France made an offer of a credit to the Bank of England for the purpose of supporting sterling, and the French Press received instructions to change its attitude.

Even during those critical days it was regarded as unthinkable in London that the British authorities should have to accept assistance from France. It was generally assumed even in well-informed banking circles that the Bank of England and the British Government would be in a position to obtain an almost unlimited amount of support in the United States. Apart from sentimental considerations, it was obviously to the interest of New York to support London to the utmost. From a political point of view, Washington regarded with growing dismay the French attempt to obtain political dictatorship in Europe by financial means. From a financial point of view, the considerable commitments of American banks in London made it desirable for the United States to assist Great Britain. From the point of view of international monetary stability, the importance of the fate of sterling was duly realised in the United States. In spite of this, when they were sounded as to their willingness to grant a substantial credit, their answer was not what was to be expected. They advised the British authorities that they could only undertake support in conjunction with France. Although their attitude was disappointing, they could not be blamed for it. It was evident that any one-sided support given by the United States would provide an opportunity for French holders of sterling, including the French authorities themselves, to withdraw their balances. As at that time the amount of French balances was estimated at about £150,000,000, it would have been necessary for the United States to provide credits well in excess of that figure in order to safeguard sterling. Owing to unsatisfactory domestic financial conditions and the severe blow which had been received as a result of the Central European difficulties, the American authorities did not feel strong enough to provide such a large amount. They advised their British friends to seek to obtain the co-operation of the French authorities, not merely in order to reduce the amount which they themselves would have to provide, but also in order to give France a material interest in the defence of sterling.

The British authorities had to recognise that, in order to save sterling, it was essential to obtain the co-operation of the French authorities. This was all the more awkward as, in consequence of the Creditanstalt incident and the subsequent clash at Basle, relations between the two central banks had become somewhat strained. Owing to the readiness with which Mr. Montagu Norman came to the rescue of the Austrian Government in defiance of France, he became the supreme object of French hatred. Systematic propaganda was carried on in the French Press and foreign newspapers inspired by French interests to undermine his authority. It was impossible for him in the circumstances to seek a *rapprochement*. At the insistence of the Court of Directors of the Bank, Sir Robert Kindersley got in touch with the Bank of France. As Sir Robert Kindersley had played a prominent part in negotiating the credit of £5,000,000 in 1924 for the support of the franc, he was *persona grata* in French official quarters, which in any case had, at this stage, become anxious to support sterling. He was informed that the Bank of France was willing to participate to the extent of 50 per cent in any assistance given, on condition that the credit should be secured by the earmarking of a corresponding amount of the Bank of

England's gold reserve. This demand was received with indignation. Had it been made public it would have roused violent opposition on the part of every section of the British Press and public opinion, and the credit could not have been concluded. Mr. Montagu Norman was known to have been opposed to the utmost to the acceptance of assistance on such humiliating terms. Indeed, for the moment there appeared to be no need for it, as, realising that the danger of a suspension of the gold standard was imminent, the Bank of France had to support sterling on its own account and at its own risk in order to prevent a further decline of the Bank of England's gold reserve. The Bank of France was buying sterling heavily; its purchases in the course of ten days were estimated at about £15,000,000. At the same time French banks were emphatically requested to refrain from any further withdrawals of funds from London. The Bank of France, however, advised the Bank of England that its voluntary support was temporary, and that its object was merely to give the Bank of England time to make up its mind about the proposed credits, and stated that unless London accepted the French terms by Friday, July 31, the Bank of France would discontinue this support, and would leave sterling to its fate. In spite of this ultimatum, many well-informed people were inclined to hold the view that in order to safeguard itself against heavy losses the Bank of France would be willing to continue to support sterling without any special arrangement. The majority of the Court of Directors of the Bank of England took, however, a different view, and overruled Mr. Norman's opposition to the terms of the French credit, which was eventually accepted before the ultimatum of the Bank of France expired.

A few days later it was announced that, for reasons of health, Mr. Montagu Norman had to take a prolonged holiday.

The next few weeks witnessed a desperate struggle to maintain the stability of sterling. The hopes, entertained by those in favour of accepting the Franco-American credit of £50,000,000, that the mere conclusion of such a credit would be sufficient to stop the flight from the pound, did not materialise. The amount was obviously inadequate to inspire confidence. According to the figures published in the Macmillan Report, the amount of London's short-termed liabilities at March 31, 1931, was £407,000,000, even without including unknown but probably substantial figures for sterling bills in the custody of foreign banks, and against this the amount of London's short-term claims which could be called in from foreign debtors was comparatively negligible. If we allow for the frozen credits in Germany and elsewhere, the net amount that could be withdrawn in the course of a few months could not have been much short of £300,000,000. In addition, foreign holders of British securities were also in a position to sell their holdings and to withdraw the proceeds. Thus the most conservative estimate placed the amount that could be withdrawn by foreign holders at about £500,000,000, and this does not include possible export of British capital. Against this a credit of £50,000,000 could hardly be expected to restore confidence, especially as it was believed that part of the sterling bought by the Bank of France at the end of July in support of the exchange had to be reimbursed out of the proceeds of the credit.

French Financial Diplomacy had thus obtained its end. After the announcement of the conclusion of the

Franco-American credit nobody could doubt any longer that London was incapable of granting any assistance, and that any possible assistance from New York would have to be arranged in collaboration with French financial interests. Mr. Montagu Norman, who was regarded as the chief obstacle to the complete victory of French Financial Diplomacy, was out of the way, and the Bank of England was placed under moral obligation not to take any action contrary to French interests. The first obvious result of the French victory was the refusal of London to participate in the issue of Hungarian Treasury Bonds. In consequence of this refusal the Hungarian Government was left at the mercy of France as the only source which could provide assistance to save the country from complete financial collapse. It had to accept the French political conditions; and its surrender was soon followed by the surrender of Germany and Austria over the question of the Customs Union scheme.

It was hoped in Paris that the victory could be achieved without paying the price for it. It was expected that the stability of sterling could be maintained, so that the loss of London's power and prestige would not cause any financial losses to the Bank of France and other French interests holding sterling. This assumption proved, however, to be too optimistic. France was soon to learn that it is easier to start an avalanche than to stop it.

CHAPTER XIII

FRANCE v. ITALY

To safeguard the security of France against a possible German aggression was by no means the only object of French Financial Diplomacy. Although its main effort was concentrated upon removing the possibility of any Anglo-Saxon financial support for Germany, it found time also to devote some attention to Italy. Ever since the war, and more particularly since the advent of the Fascist regime, Franco-Italian political relations had been far from satisfactory. Having obtained all she claimed from Austria, Italy was credited with coveting those parts of Southern France where the Italian population constitutes the majority. It was taken for granted in Paris, and possibly not without reason, that in a Franco-German war Italy would be on the side of Germany. For this reason French foreign policy aimed at strengthening Italy's natural enemy, Yugoslavia. With the aid of French credits, Yugoslavia was enabled to maintain an army far beyond her own financial means. In spite of this, her value as an ally of France in a possible Franco-Italian conflict was rendered problematic by the fact that Italy had succeeded in acquiring two political allies in Hungary and Bulgaria.

The main object of France's policy of favouring the Little Entente against Hungary was to increase the weight of the potential Yugoslav pressure against Italy. In case of a European war, the Hungarian forces would be kept duly engaged by Czechoslovakia and Roumania, so that Yugoslavia could concentrate comparatively substantial forces on the Italian front. It was felt, however, in Paris that this combination was not altogether satisfactory. In a European war Soviet Russia would hardly remain neutral, and the necessity for the defence of her Russian frontier would practically eliminate Roumania as a factor of importance in Central Europe. As to Czechoslovakia, her geographical position placed her at considerable disadvantage in face of a possible German-Austro-Hungarian alliance. The chances were, therefore, that the major part of Yugoslavia's forces would be tied down on the Hungarian and Bulgarian fronts, and Italy would have practically a free hand to concentrate her forces against France.

Although the above excursion into the field of politics may appear out of place in a book dealing with financial warfare, it is necessary to appreciate the position in order to understand the French financial attitude towards Hungary. In order to improve her chances of obtaining the effective support of Yugoslavia it was essential for France to isolate Italy and to win over her allies, especially Hungary. The financial crisis in Central Europe provided an excellent opportunity for achieving this object.

As we have seen in Chapter XI., Hungary was affected by the German crisis to a greater extent than any other country. Her troubles began as a result of the Creditanstalt crisis, owing to the close association of one of her leading banks, the Hungarian General Credit Bank, with the Creditanstalt. The latter's difficulties resulted in a run on the Hungarian General

Credit Bank, and foreign credits to that bank, as well as to other Hungarian houses, were called in on a large scale. To overcome the difficulties the National Bank succeeded in obtaining a small short-term credit through the Bank for International Settlements. This arrangement was, however, insufficient to consolidate the position, and the Hungarian Government began to negotiate the issue of £5,000,000 of eighteen months Treasury Bonds in foreign markets. During the second half of June and the first half of July the attention of international bankers was focussed upon Germany, and the Hungarian negotiations did not make much progress. The hopes entertained in Budapest that London would provide the greater part of the credit did not materialise. By that time banking circles in London had realised that, far from being able to assist others, they themselves might have to apply for assistance. For this reason alone the chances of placing a Hungarian loan in London were anything but favourable. Moreover, in July it was becoming increasingly evident that London could not afford to repeat her gesture of June 17, when she went to the rescue of Austria in defiance of French interests. Well-informed quarters realised that part of the assistance that London might require would have to come from Paris. It was inevitable, therefore, that France would have to be allowed a free hand to deal with Hungary.

France was willing to help Hungary—at a price. Her aim was to obtain the dissolution of the Hungarian alliance with Italy and to improve Hungary's relations with the Little Entente. At the same time the Quai d'Orsay revived an old favourite plan—that of the restoration of the Austro-Hungarian monarchy under the Habsburgs. It was hoped that by such means it would be possible definitely to separate Austria from Germany. This would mean killing two birds with one stone. Naturally enough the Little Entente was anything but enthusiastic for the restoration of the Austro-Hungarian monarchy, but in the urgency of the crisis France had the means of overcoming their objections. The countries of the Little Entente were in need of financial support so as to counteract the repercussions of the crisis in Central Europe. Banks in Czechoslovakia, Yugoslavia, and Roumania experienced severe runs, and a crisis would have been inevitable but for the financial assistance of France. In such circumstances the Governments of these countries were more inclined to allow themselves to be convinced by the French argument that it was to their interest to agree to the new French policy with regard to Hungary. No immediate steps were taken, but France is believed to be waiting for an opportune moment for the restoration of the Habsburg monarchy under French auspices.

In Budapest it was hoped until the last minute that Italy would provide financial assistance, and that there would be no need for buying French help with political concessions. In fact, early in July, Italian financial interests made certain informal promises to that effect. Although Italy has never been a lending country in the real sense of the term, during the previous few years her banks had participated on several occasions in international loan transactions. In almost every case there was a political motive behind the decision to participate. Italy wanted to follow the example of the French Financial Diplomacy, though owing to her lack of financial resources the extent to which she was able to assist other countries financially for political purposes was limited. As the alliance with Hungary was the cornerstone of Italian policy in Central Europe, it was reasonable to assume that Signor Mussolini would do his utmost to maintain this alliance even at the cost of financial sacrifices. With the aggravation of the international financial crisis, however, it was becoming increasingly difficult for Italy to substitute herself for London or Paris in taking over the main portion of the Hungarian loan. The Italian commitments in Germany were comparatively moderate, and the extent to which she was affected by the German crisis was not excessive, but Italian banks were involved considerably in the difficulties of the Austro-Hungarian succession states. Moreover, the rapid development of the crisis made it appear advisable for her to conserve all her resources. Subsequent events justified this precaution, as in September and October the Italian authorities needed all their resources to defend the lira against speculative attacks.

By the middle of August the Hungarian Government realised that its only hope of obtaining the loan was to accept whatever terms France dictated. The financial situation of the country was becoming desperate, and a complete collapse appeared imminent. The number of those who urged the Government to break with its policy aiming at the restoration of pre-war Hungary, and to adapt its attitude to French requirements, was growing steadily. It was obvious that the old policy could not possibly produce any immediate results, as isolated action by Hungary against the Little Entente would have been doomed to failure, and that Hungary's only chance of recovering any part of her lost territories was through participation in another European war, which might not materialise for some decades. Meanwhile Hungary was faced with financial problems vital to her existence. Had she rejected the French claims, economic collapse would have been inevitable. The temptation to submit to French political pressure in order to escape economic disaster was too strong to be resisted. On August 17 it was announced that Count Bethlen's Government had resigned, and that Count Károlyi, who is credited with pro-French sentiments, had been entrusted by Governor Horthy with the formation of a new cabinet.

As in Austria in June 1931, so in Hungary, France attempted to obtain the maximum possible result at the least possible cost. Of the amount of the loan of £5,000,000, £1,000,000 was to be taken up by the Hungarian banks, while of the remaining £4,000,000 France took over nearly £2,400,000, the remainder being distributed amongst Italian, Swiss, and Dutch banks. Even this £4,000,000 was not paid over in cash to the Hungarian Government. Certain claims against Hungarian banks had to be deducted from it, so that the net amount actually received by Hungary was very small. Such was Hungary's plight that she was unable to refuse this arrangement even though the extent of the relief provided was inadequate. The French Minister in Budapest received a high decoration from his Government, and not without reason. He had succeeded in obtaining the dissolution of the Hungarian-Italian alliance at the cost of a short-term credit of insignificant amount.

The financial collapse in Hungary was averted, but only for the moment. Conditions remained desperate, and the existence of the country remained dependent upon further French support. This was in accordance with the plans of the French Financial General Staff.

After all, if Hungary were assisted to a sufficient extent to make any further help superfluous, she might recover her freedom of action in the sphere of International Politics, and Paris is well aware that foreign policy cannot be based upon mere gratitude. France was willing to continue to support Hungary provided that she was allowed to establish a close control over Hungarian affairs. Although it would assume the form of financial supervision to safeguard the interests of creditors, there was no doubt as to its political nature.

While French Financial Diplomacy focussed its attention upon Hungary, it did not forget Bulgaria, the second ally of Italy. Conditions in that country also were very bad, and her Government sought in vain to obtain external assistance. It was expected that the Bulgarian Government would apply for a loan at the League of Nations meeting in September 1931. M. Molloff, the Finance Minister of Bulgaria, stated, however, that his Government would prefer to forego the assistance of the League, and to establish direct contact with French banking interests. Past experience has shown that the apparatus of the League for financial assistance is too slow and complicated to be useful in emergency. By the time a loan proposal goes through the various committees, sub-committees, etc., and is approved by the Council, the country in need of assistance will probably have either recovered or collapsed. In the past, the Bank of England had usually granted an advance on prospective League of Nations loans. Owing to the changed conditions, however, she was no longer in a position to do so. It was not surprising, therefore, that Bulgaria preferred to deal directly with French banks. Once she satisfied the required political conditions she would obtain the loan without further delay. Meanwhile she could obtain an advance on it to enable her to carry on. The isolation of Italy was thus complete. France had succeeded in winning over the two countries whose alliance with Italy would have reduced the value of Yugoslav support. Italy suffered a complete defeat in the sphere of International Politics owing to the superior financial strength of France, and the skill with which the latter employed it for political purposes.

CHAPTER XIV

EUROPE'S FINANCIAL DICTATOR

AFTER our digression to the "South-Eastern front" of the French financial campaign, we may return to the main battlefield. As was to be expected, the arrangement of a credit of £50,000,000 for the Bank of England did not solve the problem of sterling. The amount was much too small to allay the fears of foreign holders of sterling balances, or to discourage bear speculation in sterling, which assumed considerable dimensions in August. The pressure against sterling continued, and the banks which were in charge of supporting the exchange had to draw extensively upon the dollar and franc credits day after day to prevent a depreciation. Within a few weeks the credits were exhausted. Negotiations had been initiated for obtaining additional assistance, and after the formation of the National Government a second credit of £80,000,000 was concluded. This time it was not a credit to the Bank of England but to the Treasury, and France and the United States participated in it in equal proportions. Although the gold reserve at the Bank was not pledged as a security for this credit, there was some understanding that the gold should be regarded as a kind of moral security. In spite of this understanding, however, the terms of the credit were extremely harsh. The lenders had every reason to be satisfied with its yield, considering the blameless record of the British Government as a debtor. High rates of interest and good security were not, however, all that France was aiming at. Although in the course of the negotiations political conditions were not mentioned—and, indeed, it is unthinkable that the British Government would have accepted a credit at the price of abandoning its political independence—it was taken for granted in France that the conclusion of the credit implied a change in Great Britain's external policy. While official quarters were diplomatic enough not to express any opinion on the subject, the French Press was unanimous in demanding that financial co-operation should be associated with political co-operation. In other words, France expected of Great Britain that for the sake of financial support she would stand aside and allow France a free hand in Germany, or possibly even actively support the French foreign policy.

Even after the conclusion of the second credit, and after the introduction of drastic budgetary measures, pressure against sterling continued. It was obvious that before very long the second credit would also be exhausted, and that, in order to avoid a collapse of sterling, it would soon be necessary to negotiate for a third credit. Meanwhile the attitude of the French Press became almost intolerable. Apart from the demand that the financial support should be connected with concessions in the sphere of foreign politics, it began to claim the right to interfere even in Britain's domestic affairs. The proposal of a revenue tariff and the unofficial suggestion of an embargo on the import of luxury articles as emergency measures to save sterling, resulted in an outburst of violent attacks in the French Press. It was openly stated that the British Government could not expect any French support unless it undertook to abstain from any measures, however necessary for the support of sterling, that might tend to damage French interests. This was the price France demanded for her financial assistance to Great Britain. It may be well to remember this when examining the true merits of the French support.

At the same time French financial warfare made further progress in Central Europe. Both Austria and Germany had to realise that there was no hope of any support elsewhere than from Paris. In both countries the memories of the disastrous effects of inflation were still too fresh, and their Governments were determined to avoid the recurrence of the calamity at all costs. They realised that they could not afford to disobey the French demand for dropping the Customs Union scheme. They reluctantly decided, therefore, to abandon the scheme even before the decision of the Hague International Court was announced. On the occasion of the meeting of the League of Nations Assembly at Geneva the Austrian and German Governments made a declaration that they would not proceed further with the project. Although the terms of their declaration did not altogether satisfy the French Government, which wished them to make a binding undertaking to abandon the scheme for ever, it constituted, nevertheless, a victory of first-rate importance for French Financial Diplomacy.

Towards the middle of September it appeared as if France had succeeded in obtaining her end. Her financial victory seemed to be complete. Amidst a world clamouring for assistance she monopolised the only source from which assistance could possibly be forthcoming. London's financial power was paralysed; she was unable to play an active part in the sphere of International Finance. In fact, she had to fight for the safety of the pound, and she was also dependent upon French assistance. New York had to struggle with her own problems, and her only desire was to keep aloof from Europe as much as possible. In spite of the continuous increase in the American gold stock there was no likelihood of any support from that quarter, and in any case New York would not undertake anything without the co-operation of Paris. The minor continental financial centres, Holland, Switzerland, and Sweden, were themselves on the defensive. The excessive German commitments of Dutch and Swiss bankers had for some time eliminated them as a potential source of support. Sweden also was in an awkward position owing to the wholesale repatriation of Swedish securities exported during the past few years. Her authorities had to look towards Paris for a credit to save the stability of the krone.

Even Soviet Russia showed an inclination to be influenced by the French financial victory. It was obvious that in the changed circumstances she could not expect any substantial credits from Germany or Great Britain. In the past credits granted to the Soviet by Germany were financed indirectly by London, New York, and other lending centres. In future there was no hope of continuing this practice. For this reason the Soviet Government considered it advisable to initiate a *rapprochement* with France in the hope of obtaining credits. Negotiations for a treaty of non-aggression between the French Republic and the U.S.S.R. have reached an advanced stage. France would undoubtedly be prepared to pay the price for securing the neutrality of Soviet Russia in case of a Franco-German war. In spite of Russia's default on pre-war debts, therefore, through which France suffered more than any other country, it would not be surprising to witness France granting new Russian loans.

The ambitions of French Financial Diplomacy had thus been realised. France had obtained the position of the financial dictator of Europe. This position carried immense political power. Were France the only country armed to the teeth in a disarmed world her political power could not have been any greater. In fact, in the changed post-war conditions she stood a better chance of attaining her political ends through financial than through military means. Any increase of her armed forces would have led to an armament race, and it would have resulted in her political isolation amidst a hostile world. The position of financial dictatorship is regarded, however, as less provocative than that of military dictatorship. While Europe and the world would have revolted against the latter, the former hardly aroused any protest. Although there appeared occasionally headlines about "France's golden bullets" in the popular Press, French financial Imperialism did not receive the attention it deserved.

The other side of the picture was a deepening of the effects of the world crisis upon the French economic situation. The drastic fiscal measures introduced by Great Britain, in order to balance her budget and to save sterling, reduced the spending power of the British public which has always been France's best customer. The French hotel industry and luxury trades were beginning to suffer in consequence. Their complaints, however, were drowned in the general pæan of triumph over the country's financial victory. With its essentially political mentality, the French nation was willing to put up with economic inconveniences for the sake of political advantages. This fact is not adequately understood abroad. It has become a stock phrase in certain British and foreign newspapers that France is beginning to realise the burdens of her golden hoard. The British Labour Party began in September to advocate an international gold conference on the assumption that France would be only too willing to co-operate so as to escape the economic consequences of her gold-hoarding policy. This assumption was based on a complete ignorance of French mentality. Far from being worried by her excessive gold supply, France was just beginning to enjoy her newly acquired wealth and power. Every new consignment of gold which entered the Bank of France was regarded with pride and satisfaction as yet another addition to France's political and financial strength. It is true that France did not remain immune from the crisis. In September signs of coming financial troubles became noticeable. Several industrial and financial concerns got into difficulties and had to be saved by official support. All these symptoms, however, were not sufficiently grave to counterbalance the satisfaction felt over the political triumph won by financial weapons. In the circumstances, to expect France to relinquish any part of her financial power in order to assist other countries, without receiving the price for it in the form of political advantages, implies an extreme optimism entirely unwarranted by past experience or by the present situation. It is not until France realises that her financial victory may lead to her political isolation that hopes of a change in her attitude may reasonably be entertained.

CHAPTER XV

SUSPENSION OF THE GOLD STANDARD

THERE is an old-fashioned card game, called "Ombre", in which the player who holds no trumps is in a stronger position than the player who holds them all. It sometimes happens that the man who holds all the trumps, and triumphantly declares *"grandissimo"*, is defeated by an opponent who unassumingly declares *"nullissimo"*. It was just in such a way that the cards of International Finance were called in September of 1931.

Towards the middle of September it was becoming more and more obvious that France held all the trumps and Great Britain none. France's gold stock was approaching half a milliard pounds while Great Britain's was barely over £130,000,000, and that was barely sufficient to cover the Franco-American credits which were being consumed in the hopeless task of defending sterling. The French authorities still held some £100,000,000 of short-term balances in London and a great deal more in New York. The British authorities were using up rapidly the foreign exchange supply obtained in part at the price of pledging their gold reserve. The French authorities were in a position to distribute rewards and punishments amongst their friends and enemies. They could save or wreck countries by granting or withholding support. Great Britain was unable to help anybody, and even her own stability depended upon external assistance. France was willing to continue to help her, but the price was the independence of Great Britain's foreign policy. But, even if the stability of the pound could have been saved at that price, the result would not have been worth the sacrifice. The British nation would have lost more in prestige and self-respect if she had sold her independence for the sake of financial support. But the dilemma did not arise. Sterling was doomed, and any support France might have cared to grant at that late stage would have only prolonged its agony without affecting its fate in the long run.

It was obviously against the interest of France for sterling to collapse. Her financial triumph was complete when London was forced to be on the defensive and ceased to be able to help others. The ideal solution from a French point of view would have been to maintain the situation as it was in August 1931, when sterling was maintained with the aid of Franco-American credits. France was willing to continue to grant further credits because she realised the disadvantages which a depreciation of sterling would entail for her, and it was obviously to her interest, political, financial, and commercial, to prevent the suspension of the gold standard in Great Britain. The anticipated effect of a depreciation of sterling on French trade was in itself a sufficient inducement for the French authorities to do their utmost to prevent such a calamity. In addition, the Bank of France's holding of sterling was considerable, and it stood to suffer severe losses on a depreciation. From a political point of view it was obvious that, once Great Britain was off the gold standard, there would be no more hope for France to influence British foreign policy.

This explains the willingness with which France granted credits to the British authorities on two occasions and was prepared to grant a third credit on the eve of the suspension of the gold standard. No gratitude is due for this belated support. After all, it was largely in consequence of the French policy of financial warfare that the position of sterling became critical, and it was not until the work of destruction had been carried too far that France began to think of checking it. The credits of £65,000,000 granted by France to the Bank of England and the British Treasury in August did not benefit Great Britain. They merely postponed the suspension of the gold standard by about seven weeks, and on the other hand they resulted in heavy external liabilities which added to the problems that had to be faced by the British authorities during a difficult period. As it was impossible to maintain the gold standard, it might have been better to suspend it in July rather than in September. The chief beneficiaries of the French support were French holders of sterling balances, who were thereby enabled to withdraw their funds at a rate of about 124. As the amount of their withdrawals was not much less than that of the French participation in the credits, the transaction was virtually equivalent to a conversion of French sterling claims into franc claims, so as to avoid losses through a depreciation of sterling.

On September 18 the French authorities were informed that the second credit of £80,000,000 was nearly exhausted, and that the British authorities had therefore no alternative but to suspend the gold standard. An eleventh-hour attempt was made to raise a third credit. France was prepared to participate in it to the extent of £32,000,000, provided that the United

States was prepared to take up a similar amount. The answer from New York was, however, in the negative. It was realised in New York that the third credit would meet with the same fate as the first two: it would be used to bolster up an untenable position without any benefit to Great Britain in the long run.

On September 20 it was announced that it had become necessary to suspend the gold standard. This was Britain's *"nullissimo"* in answer to France's *"grandissimo"*. It was the inevitable result of the force of circumstances, but had the course been deliberately chosen it could not have been more in accordance with British interests. As is often the case, Great Britain tumbled upon the right solution by mistake. This is not the place to consider the financial and economic advantages and disadvantages of the suspension of the gold standard. Speaking purely from the point of view of international politics, it constituted a first-rate victory for Great Britain and a severe defeat for France. It is true that after the suspension of the gold standard London was not in a position to give assistance to other countries any more than she was during the period of her struggle to save sterling. On the other hand, the French hopes of dictating British foreign policy had definitely been frustrated. This explains the undisguised outburst of bad temper in Paris on receipt of the news of the suspension of the gold standard. At the moment when the triumph appeared to be complete, the suspension of the gold standard broke the spell and released Great Britain from the grip of French influence.

It has become evident that the power of French Financial Diplomacy is essentially destructive. When it was to the interest of French foreign policy to check the work of destruction, its efforts proved to be futile in the face of the adverse tendencies which it had initiated. The financial statesmen of France had to realise that, while it is easy to start an adverse trend, it is impossible to regulate it at will once it is started.

It would be, of course, a one-sided exaggeration to put the entire blame for the suspension of the gold standard upon France. Fundamental adverse factors had been at work for some time. The inelasticity of wages in Great Britain handicapped British exports, while heavy taxation, caused by the immense burden of the public debt, had brought about a steady outflow of British capital. Although she possessed about £3,500,000,000 of foreign investments, and these would normally have easily enabled sterling to stand the strain, they had been immobilised by the world crisis. As the French gold policy was largely responsible for the world crisis, France was, from this point of view, partly responsible for Great Britain's difficulties. But this was not all. France was to blame for the strain upon sterling which, during the last three years or so, had tended to deplete the Bank of England's gold reserve and was the principal cause of the undermining of confidence in the stability of sterling. The low level at which the franc was stabilised was the main cause of the gold drain, so that, even if we were prepared to admit that France was not guilty of a deliberate policy aiming at the destruction of London's financial power, she would still have to be considered responsible for the crisis of the pound.

In the light of these facts, the French attacks against Great Britain, accusing her of attempts at deliberate sabotage of the gold standard and breach of faith with holders of sterling, are too absurd to be considered seriously. France is the last country that could accuse any other country of having disappointed those who had faith in the stability of its currency.

Although it was evident that the suspension of the gold standard in Great Britain was not the result of a deliberate policy, but was decided upon under the stress of circumstances, when there was no alternative, a considerable section of public opinion in France regarded it, nevertheless, as a sinister move directed against France. It was stated in the Press in all seriousness that the aim of the British action was to wreck the gold standard all over the world, and to isolate those few countries—France and the United States in the first place—which had a sufficiently large gold reserve to retain the gold standard. In reality, however, it was obviously against the interests of Great Britain that other countries should follow her example. The beneficial effect of a depreciating exchange upon export trade would be reduced to a minimum if many other countries were to depreciate their currencies.

It did not take long for the French Financial General Staff to discover the line it had to take in the changed circumstances. By the act of suspending the gold standard Great Britain had escaped the influence of the French financial dictatorship. The aim to be pursued by French Financial Diplomacy was to restore its lost hold upon Great Britain. It was realised in Paris that, should the depreciation of sterling continue, Great Britain would be placed in a position to accumulate for herself considerable liquid reserves, in the same way as did France after 1926. She might even recapture some of the gold lost to France since 1927.

Such a development would imperil French financial dictatorship and should be prevented, if possible. To that end it appeared desirable to prevent the depreciation of sterling below the level to which it dropped during the first few days following the suspension of the gold standard. Had France succeeded in establishing co-operation with the United States in this respect, she would have undoubtedly undertaken to support sterling, and possibly even to bring about a partial recovery. As, however, the United States were not in a mood for such ventures and France was, by herself, unwilling to undertake the task, other means had to be devised. Time after time, reports were launched in the French Press stating as a definite fact that the British authorities had decided to stabilise sterling in the vicinity of 100 francs. Acting upon instructions received, French newspapers took every imaginable opportunity to publish reports to that effect at a time when, owing to the impending General Election, the British authorities could not possibly have made any plans for the stabilisation of sterling. On the occasion of Lord Reading's Paris visit in October, the French Press and foreign correspondents received information from official French quarters that the British Foreign Secretary stated that the stabilisation rate of 100 francs had been decided upon. A few days later, the French Press published an alleged interview with one of the directors of the Bank of England in which again the stabilisation rate of 100 francs was mentioned. Both statements were promptly denied, but, as is usually the case, about 50 per cent of the public believed the original statements and the other 50 per cent the denials. All the time, the French Press was unanimous in declaring the willingness of France to assist Great Britain in the attempt to stabilise the pound at 100 francs.

The stabilisation of sterling at such a high level was obviously to the interest of France, as it would have reduced her losses upon her sterling balances and also would have safeguarded the interests of French trade. There were many people in Great Britain who, for various considerations, would also have preferred to see sterling stabilised at as high a rate as possible; the French *ballon d'essai* aimed at strengthening the movement in favour of stabilising sterling at a high level. Apart from its financial and commercial advantages for France, this solution would have been in accordance with the plans of French Financial Diplomacy. If sterling were allowed to depreciate and the Bank of England were thereby enabled to accumulate a substantial foreign exchange reserve, Great Britain would become independent of French financial support. Moreover, if sterling were allowed to fluctuate for a prolonged period, the French support would not be needed during that time and could not be used as a negotiating counter for obtaining political concessions. If, on the other hand, the British authorities were to decide to stabilise at an early date and at a high level, they could not carry out their plans without French assistance. The success of the British monetary policy would depend once more upon French support, which could only be obtained at the cost of the independence of British foreign policy. Thus the victory of French political finance would be once more complete.

It is beyond the scope of this book to deal with the arguments for and against an early stabilisation of sterling, and the merits or demerits of stabilising at a high level. Whether or not it is to the advantage of Great Britain to stabilise sterling as soon as possible and as high as possible it is for the British nation to judge. Any outside attempt to influence its decision and to force the hand of those responsible for its monetary policy is to be regarded as an unwarranted interference in its domestic affairs. While such interference would be unthinkable in a political sphere, it has aroused practically no opposition in the financial sphere. Had the French Government attempted to influence the results of the General Election in Great Britain, this interference would have roused indignation and protest. But the attempt to influence the decision regarding the fate of sterling was at least as grave a case of interference as would be definite support of one of the political parties. It gives an idea of how far French Financial Diplomacy is ready to go in pursuing its objects.

CHAPTER XVI

FRANCE *v*. THE UNITED STATES

WE have seen in the previous chapter that the immediate reaction in France to the suspension of the gold standard in Great Britain was to suspect a British plot to isolate France and other countries safely established on the gold basis. The French authorities lost no time in taking steps to defend themselves against this imaginary plot. By skilful handling of the Press, it was arranged that M. Laval should receive an invitation to Washington to discuss possibilities of co-operation between France and the United States as the two principal countries on a gold basis. The idea was to form a kind of *sainte alliance* in defence of the gold standard.

Before very long, however, France realised that she was in a stronger position than the United States. It is true that the gold stock of the United States, which reached a total of five milliard dollars in September, was about twice as large as that of France, but, while France had huge balances abroad, mainly in New York, the United States had enormous short-term liabilities to foreign countries. In this respect, New York's position was somewhat similar to that of London. The amount of foreign balances held in New York was even larger than that held in London previous to the crisis. At the end of 1930 it was estimated at something like three milliard dollars, and there is every reason to believe that, during the first nine months of this year, this amount increased considerably as a result of the flight from the pound and from other currencies. It is true that the amount of American short-term credits was also considerable, but the greater part of these consisted of claims against Germany, which had been frozen since July. The second largest amount was represented by sterling balances, which could not be withdrawn after September 21 without incurring considerable losses on the exchange. Thus it may be stated safely that the net amount of the short-term liabilities of New York was somewhere between two and two-and-a-half milliard dollars at the end of September. Although the amount of American long-term capital invested abroad was a multiple of this figure, this was hopelessly frozen for the time being, just as had been the case with Great Britain. On the other hand, a large amount of American stocks and bonds was held abroad, and constituted an additional potential short-term liability. It is true that the American gold reserve at that time was quite sufficient to cover the maximum imaginable requirements for foreign withdrawals—this was the essential point in which the American situation differed from the British —but it was feared that any heavy gold withdrawals might easily cause a panic in Wall Street and might bring about a run on banks. At the same time the continuous increase in the note-hoarding at home was tending to reduce the amount of free gold available for meeting external requirements.

The dollar enjoyed the complete confidence of the world until the end of September. Most of the foreign deposits withdrawn from London after the suspension of the gold standard in Great Britain were transferred to New York, and the direction followed by the flight of British capital was also mainly to the United States. During the last few days of September, however, France began to purchase gold in New York on a large scale. Other European countries, such as Holland, Switzerland, and Belgium, followed her example, but their operations were on a smaller scale than those of France. French banks began to repatriate their dollar balances, and the exchange moved strongly in favour of France. As a result, shipments of gold from New York to Paris began on a large scale. Day after day, gold amounting to anything up to fifty million dollars was embarked, mostly for France. The amount taken was only limited by the facilities available for shipment and insurance. Within three weeks over $600,000,000 of gold was shipped to Europe.

At first the movement attracted comparatively little attention, for it was known that the United States could well afford to lose gold. Moreover, at the same time as she was shipping gold to Europe, she was receiving large amounts from South America, Canada, and the Far East. After a few days, however, when the gold movements did not subside and the dollar remained persistently below gold export point, the world began to show signs of uneasiness as to the prospects of the gold standard in the United States. The withdrawals of deposits from New York increased incessantly, and foreign holders of dollar securities began to realise their holdings and to withdraw the proceeds.

It was then realised in Paris that the hour had struck for France to assert her financial power, even against the United States. The Bank of France and the French Treasury were the principal foreign holders of dollars. Their total holding towards the middle of October was estimated at about $600,000,000. Thus it was their attitude which largely determined the development of the flight from the dollar. For months past, the Bank of France had been converting its bill holdings into sight deposits, so as to be in a position to withdraw them at a moment's notice. Considering that the rate of interest on bills was very low, the extent of the loss involved was negligible. By the end of September it was believed that practically the whole of the dollar holdings of the French authorities consisted of sight deposits. Part of them were used for earmarking gold, but, until the middle of October, the French authorities did not begin to withdraw their holdings on a large scale. On October 15 M. Farnier, Deputy-Governor of the Bank of France, accompanied by M. Lacour-Gayet, late French financial attaché in Washington, arrived in New York in order to discuss with the American authorities the question of the withdrawal of French official dollar deposits. The French Press was at pains to emphasise that the journey of the two experts was entirely unconnected with the impending Washington visit of M. Laval. It was pointed out that the reason why the French authorities were anxious to make arrangements for the withdrawal of their holding before M. Laval's arrival was to avoid the appearance of any connection between the impending Washington discussions and the withdrawal of balances. The negotiations of the representatives of the Bank of France with the Federal Reserve authorities were even represented merely as normal routine exchange of views between two business friends which were in any case always in touch with each other.

Qui s'excuse s'accuse. This somewhat premature defence against anticipated criticisms carried but little conviction. It was evident that the French Government intended to make use of its power to withdraw its balances from New York as a negotiating counter in the coming Washington discussions. The French Financial General Staff realised that it had the power to cause New York considerable inconvenience by the withdrawal of the official deposits. It was hoped that France would thus be able to dictate the external policy of the United States. President Hoover's attitude to war debts and reparations was watched with growing uneasiness at the Quai d'Orsay. It was an open secret that he intended to make proposals of much greater importance than his twelve months' debt holiday. In some quarters it was expected that he would propose the extension of the debt holiday to five years. In other quarters he was expected to suggest a radical reduction of war debts and reparations in accordance with the changed capacity of the debtor nations. In either case his proposals would have been immensely beneficial to the world, but they would have crossed the plans of French Financial Diplomacy. It was evident that such proposals would be applauded all over the world, with the exception of France, and that any attempted resistance on her part would lead to her complete political isolation. It would make the world realise that France was the sole obstacle to economic recovery: that 1,500,000,000 human beings had to continue to suffer because of the refusal of the 40,000,000 Frenchmen to give up their pound of flesh. In spite of her military and financial power, France could not possibly afford to expose herself to the unanimous hatred of the rest of the world. Her Government duly realised this, and the Financial General Staff undertook to do its utmost to prevent the development of such a situation. President Hoover would have to be prevented, at all costs, from making any sweeping proposals.

Circumstances played into the hands of French Financial Diplomacy. Anxiety as to the fate of the dollar went on increasing throughout October, and, but for the supporting transactions carried out on behalf of the Federal Reserve Bank by the Paris office of the Guaranty Trust Company, the dollar would have depreciated considerably below gold export point owing to the limitations of the facilities for gold shipments. In certain remote markets, such as Warsaw, there was a dollar panic; the public threw their dollar notes on the market at a discount of five to six per cent. In the United States itself, the nervous tension increased. There was a run on a number of small and medium-sized banks all over the country, and the number of bank failures increased to an alarming degree. At the same time, the public was hoarding notes, and the demand for Treasury gold certificates increased. There was some danger that any spectacular change, such as the wholesale withdrawal of French official deposits, might prove the last straw. From a technical point of view, the United States could well afford to repay these deposits in gold. From a psychological point of view, however, such a transaction was undesirable, as it might provoke a panic.

As has been the case with withdrawals of gold from London during the past three years, the French authorities have disclaimed any influence on the gold withdrawals from New York. It is true that the greater part of them was carried out on behalf of the American authorities themselves for the purpose of acquiring the franc balances necessary for supporting the dollar, but it is more than probable that the weakness of the dollar was due in part—directly or indirectly —to the action of the French authorities. We have seen in Chapter VI. that whenever sterling depreciated and gold was withdrawn from London, the French Bank returns always showed an increase in the balances of the French Treasury and the Caisse d'Amortissements with the Bank of France. In October, gold withdrawals from New York also coincided with such an increase. This may be interpreted in two different ways. Either it means that the French authorities contracted the resources of the French money market and thereby forced French banks to withdraw balances from abroad, or it may mean that the French Treasury and the Caisse d'Amortissements were themselves selling dollars, and the proceeds of their operations were transferred to the Bank of France. It was thus probable that the French authorities had contributed towards the adverse trend of the dollar. This was the way in which French Financial Diplomacy prepared M. Laval's Washington visit.

Towards the middle of October, the time arrived for French Financial Diplomacy to deliver the masterstroke. Its main object was no longer an alliance, between countries on a gold basis, to defend the gold standard. That idea faded into the background; Paris was playing a much bigger game. She was willing to refrain from withdrawing her deposits provided President Hoover undertook to refrain from taking the initiative for the revision of war debts.

It was, of course, impossible to connect the two questions officially. Any suggestion of negotiating on such a basis would have been indignantly rejected by the United States administration. French Financial Diplomacy was subtle enough to realise that different situations require different methods. In the case of Austria, they could afford to discard every pretence and suggest financial assistance at the price of political concessions. In the case of the United States, they had to be more diplomatic.

M. Farnier, who is regarded as the moving spirit of the French financial warfare, handled his task with supreme skill. On his arrival in New York a day before M. Laval's departure for Washington, he informed the American monetary authorities that the Bank of France was anxious to avoid the recurrence of its experience with its sterling balances, and that unless the exchange rate of its dollar balances were guaranteed, it would have to withdraw them. Incidentally, he also demanded better interest rates on the French official deposits, and suggested that to that end the New York Bank rate should be raised to $4\frac{1}{2}$ per cent, —an unprecedented interference with the domestic affairs of another country. At the same time, he stated his intention of transferring some $200,000,000 of the French official deposits from private banking interests to the Federal Reserve Bank. A tentative arrangement was reached as to the amount of deposits which should be left in New York, but M. Farnier made it plain that this agreement would have to form part of a general agreement that might be concluded in Washington between President Hoover and M. Laval. In plain English, unless President Hoover accepted M. Laval's terms, the French authorities would not hesitate to cause extreme inconvenience to New York by withdrawing their deposits.

Although MM. Laval and Farnier were after big game they did not hesitate to pick up incidentally the small fry that came their way. The fact that in the midst of the world crisis the Bank of France endeavoured to increase its profits by forcing the Federal Reserve Bank to raise its discount rate is characteristic of the destructive policy pursued by France. It is a commonplace of economic text-books that a rise in interest rates tends to accentuate the fall of prices, or to check a rising trend. The French authorities would not hesitate for the sake of an additional yield of about five million dollars to inflict damages upon producers and holders of stocks all over the world amounting to at least as many milliards or to frustrate hopes for an economic recovery through a rise of prices.

Banking interests in New York were not particularly frightened by M. Farnier's concealed threat. His demand for a higher deposit rate was unanimously rejected, and the views were expressed that New York would be better off without the French deposits. The monetary authorities were inclined to take a different view, because of the possible effect of French withdrawals upon the attitude of other foreign holders of dollars, who would be likely to follow the lead of France. It was obvious that, whatever arrangement could be reached, the ultimate result would depend upon the outcome of M. Laval's negotiations at Washington.

It is as yet premature to determine how far French Financial Diplomacy has succeeded in attaining its end. President Hoover is said to have agreed to make no further move in the matter of war debts and reparations without consulting France in advance. This constitutes a valuable victory for France, and is certainly worth the price paid for it by leaving the official deposits in New York—especially as the problem of higher yield and guaranteed exchange is also said to have been solved. But the willingness of President Hoover to consult France in advance does not in itself curtail his freedom of action. It would be, indeed, unthinkable that a great nation such as the United States should yield to French political blackmail, and, for the sake of retaining deposits of some $600 millions, submit to dictation in a matter of foreign policy of vital importance to the United States and to the rest of the world. Such a submission would do infinitely more harm to the prestige of the nation than would a suspension of the gold standard. It is, moreover, by no means certain, even if the United States Government were willing to humiliate itself to such a degree, that the favour obtained would be of any lasting benefit. For, if the French policy leads to a collapse in Germany—whether in the form of a complete moratorium or a suspension of the gold standard—the repercussions upon her principal creditor, the United States, might produce a much more damaging effect than the withdrawal of French deposits.

The attitude of the United States within the next few months will indicate whether France has succeeded, by means of financial pressure, in diverting her from the path of the constructive Anglo-Saxon policy. It is impossible to imagine that the American nation would choose a course which, as recently as three months before the Washington meeting, was indignantly rejected by Austria.

CHAPTER XVII

BALANCE-SHEET OF THE FINANCIAL WAR

At the time of writing, the financial warfare conducted by France against the rest of the world is still in progress. It would be premature, therefore, to speak of its definite results. It is, none the less, possible and desirable to examine the value to France of the results hitherto obtained, and to compare them with the price which she has paid for them so far and is likely to pay in the future.

The following is a summary of the credit side of the balance-sheet:

(1) Germany has been reduced to a state where her economic stability depends upon French goodwill.

(2) The Austro-German Customs Union scheme has been frustrated.

(3) France has obtained full control of political developments in the Succession States of the Austro-Hungarian Monarchy.

(4) Italy has been politically isolated, her allies having been won over by France.

(5) Great Britain has been reduced to a state where she is unable to grant any assistance to other countries against the wishes of France.

(6) The United States has relinquished in favour of France the privilege of taking the initiative in any action with a view to solving the problem of war debts and reparations.

(7) France has acquired a monopolistic position in the sphere of International Finance as the only potential source of assistance.

(8) Paris has become for the time being the principal international financial centre.

The question is how far these advantages are of a lasting character. It is obvious that France can only maintain her monopolistic position in the sphere of International Finance while the world crisis continues to paralyse the financial forces of Great Britain and the United States. The external investments of both these countries are considerably larger than those of France; but, while France possesses her resources in a liquid form, most of the resources of Great Britain and the United States are at present immobilised. A gradual economic recovery would release these frozen assets. Unless there is complete economic collapse and chaos, the capital invested by Great Britain and the United States in foreign countries will become recoverable sooner or later. It is only a question of time before Great Britain and the United States will be in a position to release part of their assets and acquire once more liquid resources available for the support of other nations. But, apart altogether from this, an improvement in the trade balance of either of these two countries would, in itself, tend to create new liquid resources. There is every reason to hope that, as a result of the depreciation of sterling, the British trade balance will produce a substantial export surplus during the next few years and that this, together with the repatriation of British capital which took flight abroad, will place at the disposal of the London market considerable liquid resources, with the aid of which Great Britain may once more play an active part in the sphere of International Finance.

Thus the chances are that, sooner or later, Germany will cease to depend for existence upon the good graces of France. This fact is, in itself, sufficient to reduce the value, in the long run, of the achievement of French Financial Diplomacy. Any promise or agreement forced upon Germany in the present circumstances will become of doubtful value once the circumstances which compelled Germany to accept them have ceased to exist. The same is true of the French political influence in other parts of the Continent. As soon as the Governments which reluctantly submitted to French political dictation are able to receive financial assistance from other sources, they are likely to revert to the policy which they suspended for the sake of French support. The elaborate arrangements planned in Central Europe to safeguard French political interests will then collapse like a house of cards.

But, even if we were to suppose that, thanks to the French financial victory, the world will have to suffer a prolonged period of economic depression, this does not necessarily mean that France can maintain her political influence by financial means for any length of time. Her financial resources are, after all, not inexhaustible. The chances are that, in the course of the next few years, these resources will decline rather than increase. The French trade balance, which showed a surplus for some years as a result of the stabilisation of the franc at a low level, became strongly adverse in 1931. It seems highly probable that the adverse balance will increase in the course of the next few years, for, as a result of the general depression, the demand for French luxury exports will decline, and tourist traffic in France will be reduced to a minimum. The appreciation of the franc against other currencies will also tend to check exports and encourage imports. In consequence of the default of a number of debtor countries, French investors stand to suffer to the same extent as British or American investors, and, moreover, there is not the least likelihood of Germany resuming full reparations payments. All these circumstances together make it inevitable that French financial resources will tend to decline.

At the same time France will have to continue to support the countries which belong to her political sphere of influence or have come within her influence under the pressure of financial crisis. She will have to continue to support her natural allies: Poland, Roumania, Czechoslovakia, and Yugoslavia. It is only thanks to French support that these countries have been able to avoid crises similar to those of Germany and Hungary, and the danger is by no means over. From time to time we read that France has had to grant fresh support to one or other of these countries. In addition, France will have to spend considerable amounts on maintaining her newly acquired political influence in Central Europe. Although she won her victory at a very low cost, the amount of credit she granted to Austria and Hungary was only the initial expense. In order to maintain her influence, she will have to extend additional loans and credits to both these countries. The moment she ceases to satisfy their requirements, the political financial links that join them to France will cease to exist. Over and above everything else, France will have to pay a heavy price for maintaining her financial influence over Germany. At present, the German authorities are fighting a desperate battle against the forces which threaten to bring about a financial collapse. They are determined to avoid inflation at all costs, and may even accept French political dictation as the price of financial support. Should their efforts fail, however, a collapse of the reichsmark is certain to bring about a complete political upheaval in Germany. It is highly probable that either the extreme Nationalists or the Communists will then acquire power. In either case, the French political influence over Germany would cease. It is thus evidently to the interest of France to do her utmost to prevent a complete collapse of the reichsmark. Should the situation become critical, it would be necessary for France to grant substantial support to prevent a repetition of the collapse of 1923.

The total liquid resources of France are estimated at about £800,000,000 at gold parity. It may be assumed that, in the course of the next two years or so, natural adverse tendencies will result in a reduction of these resources by about £150 to £200 millions, while a certain amount will have to be spent in order to maintain the results of the French financial victory. Thus, by the end of 1933, the fighting fund will probably be somewhere between £500 and £600 millions at par. It is still a considerable figure, but leaves only a comparatively small margin for further financial support. Before very long, the moment may arrive when France will find herself no longer in a position to continue to meet the demand for assistance. The moment she has to refuse fresh applications, the spell will be broken.

If France expects gratitude for past financial support, and if she expects that the allegiance of her new allies will continue after she has ceased to be able to pay the price for it, she will soon be disillusioned. Political influence at the price of financial support can only be maintained by continuing that support indefinitely, and this is more than any nation can afford.

Although for the present Paris may enjoy the passing glory of being the world's chief financial centre, sooner or later she will learn the inconveniences attached to that distinction. At present considerable amounts of foreign capital are being placed in France, as she is regarded as the most stable country. This process may continue for some time, and may further increase the financial power of France, but a time is bound to come when these foreign funds will be withdrawn. A war scare on the Continent will be sufficient to induce most foreign holders of French balances and securities to transfer their funds to other countries. Although at the present moment France could well afford to pay them out without any inconvenience, a situation may arise when such withdrawals may be as inconvenient to her as they were to Austria in May and June 1931, to Germany in June and July, to Great Britain in August and September, and to the United States in September and October. As the French public is extremely nervous, it is probable that any wholesale withdrawal of foreign funds would result in a heavy efflux of French capital, which would further aggravate the consequences of the withdrawal. Thus the capital influx, which is at present an additional source of financial strength, may well prove to be a danger to the financial stability of France.

We have seen that the assets in the balance-sheet

of the financial war are essentially of a temporary nature. Let us now examine the liabilities. The following is a summary of the losses which France has incurred as the price of her financial victory:

(1) France has ruined her chances of ever receiving any substantial amount of reparations.

(2) The French nation is bound to suffer through the repercussions of the world economic crisis to an increasing extent.

(3) She is bound to suffer losses, sooner or later, on the political loans granted.

(4) She has lost the sympathy of Great Britain and other nations, which would have safeguarded her against any possible German aggression.

Most of the funds which France has received from Germany in reparations have been raised by German loans and credits in London, New York, and other countries. As a result of the developments during the second half of 1931, there is no chance whatever of the resumption of German borrowing abroad for some time. It is certain that no German loan can ever be raised abroad so long as reparations are not cancelled. As Germany has been reduced to a state where her financial stability is in danger, insistence by France on reparations payments would bring about a collapse which would further remove all possibility of such payments being effected.

It has been believed in Paris that France would be able to escape the repercussions of the economic crisis, for which she is mainly responsible. Unquestionably, up to now, the extent of these repercussions has been comparatively moderate. There have been a few bank failures, while other banks have had to be reconstructed at a considerable sacrifice. Depression prevails in the textile trade and other branches of production. Agriculture suffers as a result of low prices. The hotel industry is beginning to feel the consequences of the crisis. But, comparatively speaking, the depression has affected France to a much smaller extent than almost any other country. There is no reason to suppose, however, that this state of affairs will continue. There are distinct signs that indicate a tendency towards the rapid aggravation of the crisis in France. Although she may be more self-sufficient than most other nations, she will soon realise that she cannot remain prosperous in a crisis-stricken world. Her own nationals seem to have no confidence in her financial stability. There is a persistent withdrawal of deposits from banks, and the hoarding of notes has assumed unprecedented dimensions. Even the stability of the franc is viewed with distrust by the French population, as is shown by the extent to which gold coins and gold bars are being bought at a premium. Should this wave of distrust become accentuated as a result of the aggravation of the crisis, it would paralyse all banking activity and would reduce France to a state hardly better than that of other countries.

The pre-war methods of political finance cost French investors milliards of francs through the default of Russia and other countries. Sooner or later France will learn another lesson on the financial disadvantages of combining politics with finance. It is doubtful whether the amounts lent by France to her political allies for armament purposes will ever be repaid, while the price paid for the conclusion of new alliances may also be counted amongst the doubtful assets. The financial cost of the politico-financial victory will be, in the long run, larger than is at present suspected.

As a result of the destruction caused by the French financial warfare, France is losing rapidly the sympathy she enjoyed abroad. While, during the first few years after the war, any fresh attack upon her would have rallied all her late allies in her defence, at present she could only expect support from the Little Entente and Poland. France has come to be regarded as Germany was regarded before 1914: as the principal danger to real peace. The conception is gaining ground that she has forfeited her rights to reparations by the destructive use she has made of her claims. In fact, it is now widely held that it is France who owes the world reparations for the damages caused by her destructive financial warfare. History has proved that no nation can afford to remain in isolation for any length of time. Thus the financial victory has not brought to France her much desired security from aggression; on the contrary, it has weakened the moral forces that would have otherwise guaranteed her safety.

Undoubtedly France would gladly pay the cost of her financial victory if, in return, she should obtain permanent security from aggression; but this will not be the case. Although, for the moment, she need not fear an attack, this is not the achievement of her Financial Diplomacy, as, in any case, there was no likelihood of aggression in the near future. Taking a long view, she is less safe against aggression than she was before her financial victory, for she has lost the sympathies of all nations on whose support she could previously have relied.

CHAPTER XVIII

FUTURE PROSPECTS

THE French financial warfare has resulted in complete chaos in the sphere of International Finance, and has been largely responsible for an economic crisis without precedent in modern history. Perhaps the worst of it is yet to come. Nobody can foresee the development of the situation; every day may have a new calamity in store. It is possible that the price-level in countries which have remained on a gold basis will continue to fall. Chaotic currency conditions will also add to the world's difficulties, and it is highly probable that the general economic situation will become further aggravated. According to extreme pessimists, the crisis will lead to a complete collapse of civilisation; according to others, it will result in the substitution of the Capitalist system by Communism. Others are a shade less pessimistic: they merely expect a return to more primitive conditions all over the world. All these views may be exaggerated, but it is beyond doubt that, for generations, the world will have to continue to pay a heavy price for the French financial warfare. Unless genuine international co-operation is established, the recovery from the present crisis is bound to be a slow and painful process. Every nation will try to work out its own salvation at the expense of the others, and the whole international economic system will break up into isolated units.

A few months were sufficient to destroy an immense amount of confidence accumulated during a century of comparative stability. If the work of destruction is allowed to take its full course, it will take another century before this confidence is restored. Unless the destructive tendencies are checked soon, the public will lose all confidence in banks and currencies. Everybody will demand the return of gold coins into circulation, and this would tend to accentuate the fall of prices still further. As the demand could not be fully satisfied, a primitive form of barter might take the place of our highly developed monetary system. From a political point of view, the good work of pacifist currents will suffer a set-back. Misery and despair in Germany and other countries may reach such a pitch that they will drive nations into war as the only apparent way to escape suffering. Class struggles in various countries may develop into civil war, and provide an excellent opportunity for Moscow to fish in the troubled waters.

The question is, What is to be done to avert complete disaster? The main causes of the economic deadlock are the French attitude towards reparations, the maldistribution of gold, and the French ambitions to rule Europe by means of her financial power. The first two are closely associated with the third, as neither the problem of reparations nor the world's gold problem can be solved without the wholehearted co-operation of France. It is, therefore, obvious that the termination of the financial warfare is the indispensable condition of an economic recovery. To reassure the world, it is necessary to find a definite solution for war debts and reparations. Half measures and provisional arrangements would be unable to dispel the atmosphere of uncertainty which at present effectively prevents any substantial and lasting recovery. It is equally necessary to bring about an equitable redistribution of gold. That, in itself, may not work all the miracles some people expect of it. But, as it implies genuine co-operation, it would go a long way towards restoring confidence.

The key to the situation lies with France. Without her co-operation, in the true sense of the term, there is no hope of obtaining an immediate redistribution of the world's gold supplies. Unfortunately, France is still far from realising the necessity for changing her attitude. She hopes that her huge gold hoard will make her immune from the effects of the world crisis and that her financial power will provide her with permanent security against aggression. Her disillusionment is only a question of time. If she persists in her policy, she is bound to realise her mistake within the next few years. But meanwhile the world will have to go on suffering.

For the present, there are, unfortunately, no signs to indicate any desire for financial disarmament on the part of France. Those who expect her to make a magnanimous gesture in the near future are unduly optimistic. The whole attitude of the French Press and of the official representatives of France indicates that France is less inclined than ever to co-operate. Having succeeded in eliminating British and American financial and political influence from the Continent, she is at last in a position to take full advantage of the weapon of her reparations policy, and she shows no inclination to relinquish it any more than the political power of her hoarded gold. It is maintained in Paris that all the gold France possesses is needed for her own requirements. Should the crisis in France become aggravated, this will certainly become true, for the hoarding of gold and of notes by the French population will assume high proportions, and it will considerably reduce the amount available for redistribution. Thus, while at present France would be in a position, with a little goodwill, to render a great service to the world, within a few months this may no longer be the case.

In order to avert a complete collapse and to set a recovery in motion, it is of vital importance that France should be made to realise the grave consequences of her policy. So long as she imagines that financial dictatorship is in accordance with the interests of her security, no economic or financial arguments against it will carry any weight in the eyes of French politicians or the French nation. It is necessary to make France realise that her policy is leading to her political isolation and that, consequently, it endangers her security. For sooner or later the intense hatred that is growing all over the world for the nation which inflicted sufferings on five continents is bound to lead to an international alliance to crush the offender.

The disaster of another war, which would complete the work of destruction, must be avoided at all costs. It may be that a *pax Romana*, imposed on the world by the military and financial legions of France, is a smaller evil than an armament race and the incessant threat of war. But it is unthinkable that twentieth-century Europe would be willing to submit for any length of time to the dictatorship of one nation. There must be some way of making France realise the consequences of her policy for herself. The coming disarmament conference is doomed to failure unless it is connected with an attempt to obtain financial disarmament, and some such attempt must be made. A plan for the solution of the world's financial troubles should be elaborated and submitted to the conference. Disarmament, a definite solution of the problem of reparations, and the redistribution of gold supplies should be connected with a proposal for a pact to secure France against aggression. With this approach co-operation for the common good might perhaps be achieved. For it is unthinkable that French statesmen should be so completely blinded by the glamour of their financial victory that they would fail to foresee what would be the consequences of a refusal to co-operate: that they would not realise, when it came to the ultimate decision, that no nation can bring the world to ruin with impunity.

THE END

Printed in Great Britain by R. & R. CLARK, LIMITED, *Edinburgh*.

INTERNATIONAL FINANCE
An Arno Press Collection

Bagehot, Walter. **Lombard Street.** 1915

Balogh, T[homas]. **The Dollar Crisis, Causes and Cure.** 1949

Beyen, J.W. **Money in Maelstrom.** 1949

Bloomfield, Arthur I. **Monetary Policy under the International Gold Standard: 1880-1914.** 1959

British Parliamentary Reports on International Finance: The Cunliffe Committee and The Macmillan Committee Reports. Two vols. in one. 1918/1931

Brown, John Crosby. **A Hundred Years of Merchant Banking.** 1909

Brown, William Adams, Jr. **England and the New Gold Standard: 1919-1926.** 1929

Cassel, Gustav. **Foreign Investments.** 1928

Chandler, Lester V. **Benjamin Strong, Central Banker.** 1958

Child, Frank C. **The Theory and Practice of Exchange Control in Germany.** 1958

Clare, George. **The ABC of the Foreign Exchanges.** Second Edition. 1895

Clay, Henry. **Lord Norman.** 1957

DeVegh, Imre. **The Pound Sterling: A Study of the Balance of Payments of the Sterling Area.** 1939

Dulles, Eleanor Lansing. **The French Franc, 1914-1928.** 1929

Einzig, Paul. **Behind the Scenes of International Finance.** 1931

Einzig, Paul. **World Finance: 1914-1935.** 1935

Gibson, Norman R. **The Case For International Money.** (Doctoral Thesis, Massachusetts Institute of Technology, 1974). 1979.

Gilbert, Milton. **Currency Depreciation and Monetary Policy.** 1939

Goschen, George J. **The Theory of the Foreign Exchanges.** Fifteen Edition. 1892

Graham, Frank D. and Charles R. Whittlesey. **Golden Avalanche.** 1939

Great Britain, Parliamentary Debates. **Report from the Select Committee on the High Price of Gold Bullion**—Ordered by the House of Commons to be Printed 8, June 1810. 1812

Gregory, T[heodor] E[manuel Gugenheim]. **The Gold Standard and Its Future.** 1932

Harris, C. R. S. **Germany's Foreign Indebtedness.** 1935

Harris, S[eymour] E. **Exchange Depreciation.** 1936

Hawtrey, R[alph] G[eorge]. **Currency and Credit.** 1919

Hidy, Muriel Emmie. **George Peabody, Merchant and Financier, 1829-1854.** (Doctoral Dissertation, Radcliffe College, 1939). 1979

Kemmerer, Edwin Walter. **Gold and the Gold Standard.** 1944
Kindleberger, Charles P. **The Dollar Shortage.** [1950]
League of Nations. **The Course and Control of Inflation.** 1946
League of Nations. **Interim Report of the Gold Delegation of the Financial Committee** *and* **Report of the Gold Delegation of the Financial Committee.** Two vols. in one. 1930/1932
League of Nations. **International Currency Experience, Lessons of the Inter-War Period.** 1944
League of Nations. **Memorandum on Currency and Central Banks, 1913-1924.** Two vols. in one. 1925
League of Nations. **Memorandum on Currency and Central Banks, 1913-1925.** Two vols. in one. Second Edition. 1926
Mackenzie, Compton. **Realms of Silver: One Hundred Years of Banking in the East.** 1954
Mantoux, Étienne. **The Carthaginian Peace or the Economic Consequences of Mr. Keynes.** 1946
Matsukata, Masayoshi. **Report on the Adoption of the Gold Standard in Japan.** 1899
Metzler, Lloyd A., Robert Triffin and Gottfried Haberler. **International Monetary Policies.** 1947
Mintz, Ilse. **Deterioration in the Quality of Foreign Bonds Issued in the United States, 1920-1930.** 1951
Morton, Walter A. **British Finance, 1930-1940.** 1943
Pandit, Y[eshwant] S. **India's Balance of Indebtedness, 1898-1913.** 1937
Polk, Judd. **Sterling: Its Meaning in World Finance.** 1956
Schacht, Hjalmar [H. G.] **The Stabilization of the Mark.** 1927
Schrecker, Ellen. **The Hired Money: The French Debt to the United States, 1917-1929.** (Doctoral Thesis, Harvard University, 1973). 1979
Shepherd, Henry L. **The Monetary Experience of Belgium: 1914-1936.** 1936
Simon, Matthew. **Cyclical Fluctuations and the International Capital Movements of the United States, 1865-1897.** (Doctoral Dissertation, Columbia University, 1955). 1979
Southard, Frank, Jr. **The Finances of European Liberation, With Special Reference to Italy.** 1946
United Nations. **International Capital Movements During the Inter-War Period.** 1949
United States Senate. **International Monetary Conference.** 1879
Viner, Jacob. **Canada's Balance of International Indebtedness: 1900-1913.** 1924
Waight, Leonard. **The History and Mechanism of the Exchange Equalisation Account.** 1939
Wallich, Henry Christopher. **Monetary Problems of an Export Economy: The Cuban Experience, 1914-1947.** 1950
White, Harry D[exter]. **The French International Accounts: 1880-1913.** 1933
Williams, John H. **Postwar Monetary Plans and Other Essays.** Third Edition. 1947